# Christian
## Perspective

# Christianity in Spiritual Perspective

## Are you sick-and-tired of being sick-and-tired?

## James A. Brettell, DMin

Brettell Publishing
Maumelle, Arkansas

Copyright © 2010 by Rev. Dr. James A. Brettell

All rights reserved. No part of this publication may be reproduced, stored in a retrieval system, or transmitted in any form or by any means, electronic, mechanical, photocopying, digital, recording or otherwise without prior written permission of the author.

ISBN-13: 978-1456338008

To Janet Shawhan Brettell, my beloved wife of 54 years, and to my children, Lee Ann, Donna Jo and Brian, all of whom have endured the pressures associated with a husband and father in the service of our Lord and Savior Jesus Christ. The theme of our family life for the last 48 years has been "what next, Lord?" Thank you Janet, Lee Ann, Donna Jo, and Brian for your unending support over all these years.

# 1 Timothy 4:15

Meditate upon these things; give thyself wholly to them; that thy profiting may appear to all. KJV

# Contents

|  |  |
|---|---|
| Dedication | iii |
| Epigraph | iv |
| Preface | vii |
| Acknowledgements | xi |

### PART I   CHRISTIANITY AND THE ANGELIC CONFLICT
1. The "Why" and "Where" Questions — 2
2. Asking the Right Question — 9

### PART II   WHAT IS CHRISTIANITY?
3. Christianity and the Big Picture — 13
4. Christianity in Historical Perspective — 19
5. Christianity and Its Goal — 24
6. Christian Maturity Defined and Described — 30
7. The Christian Walk: Formulaic or Logical Progression? — 35

### PART III   HOW THE CHRISTIAN WAY OF LIFE WORKS
8. "Operation KRRY" Is the Answer — 38
9. Do the Truth — 52
10. The Concepts of Internalization and Actualization — 54

### PART IV   THE OLD-MAN NEW-MAN IN THE CHRISTIAN WAY OF LIFE
11. Old-Man New-Man Concepts — 59
12. Old-Man New-Man Terminology and Distinctions — 62
13. Old-Man New-Man: Two Belief Systems — 64

### PART V   THE HOLY SPIRIT AND THE CHRISTIAN WAY OF LIFE
14. "In the Spirit" — 72
15. "In the Spirit" Analogies and Demonstrations — 78
16. The Fruit of the Spirit — 83
17. Who Produces the Ninefold Fruit of the Spirit? — 85
18. The Seven Manifestations of the Spirit — 90

### PART VI   AGAPE LOVE AND THE CHRISTIAN WAY OF LIFE

| | | |
|---|---|---|
| 19. | Agape Love: What Is It? | 98 |
| 20. | Agape Love, Philos Love, and Appreciation | 106 |

**PART VII  FREEDOM AND THE CHRISTIAN WAY OF LIFE**

| | | |
|---|---|---|
| 21. | The Concept of Freedom | 109 |
| 22. | Freedom and the Angelic Conflict | 115 |

**PART VIII CHRISTIANITY AND MODERN-DAY "TONGUES"**

| | | |
|---|---|---|
| 23. | Tongues, Why They Ceased in AD70 | 120 |
| | Glossary | 141 |
| | Abbreviations | 143 |
| | Endnotes | 149 |

# Preface

We live in a day-and-age that is characterized by what I respectfully refer to as the "so what," "who cares," or "whatever" generation that reduces any serious conversation about life to just that-so what? or who cares? or whatever! The implication is that everything about life is relative and there are no absolutes. They are saying that their opinion is just as good as yours or mine. This would be true if absolutes were non-existent.

Our present generation can also be characterized as an age of moral relativity. The only absolutes believed are those held by "me"-whoever "me" might be. Here's a thought to ponder. If we're told by some that there are no absolutes, does that denial not become an absolute in itself? The very denial of the existence of absolutes demonstrates the shallow thinking of the so what, who cares, or whatever generation.

"So what?" "Who really cares?" "Whatever!" These comments shouldn't be taken lightly when discussing matters of a spiritual and eternal nature. They demonstrate antipathy toward spiritual and eternal matters and view the spiritual wisdom you're attempting to impart as no more than just another religious opinion. When the absolute truths of God's Holy Word are either ignored or rejected, there remains no standard against which the thinking of human beings can be measured for the purpose of determining what is right or wrong, good or bad-hence, the world of moral relativity.

There's a strong indication that something is terribly wrong in our present generation, but not many people are getting the picture-just yet. People are departing the traditional church in great numbers. Barna Group research reports that within this decade, ending 2010, as many as 50 million individuals[1] may rely solely upon the internet to provide all of their faith-based experiences. This is a staggering figure, and a legitimate answer should be found to the question, "Why is this happening?"

Wikipedia reports that approximately 38,000 denominations[2] exist within Christendom. Suppose that each person who is dissatisfied with his present church experience determined to investigate each denomination before deciding where to get his religious instruction. How long would it take before a final decision would be made to unite? It certainly wouldn't be soon.

How prepared are you and I to give spiritual direction to the so what, who cares, whatever crowd? To put everything into perspective for them, we as born-again Christians must stand on the absolutes of biblical truth and be able to accurately articulate the big-picture of human history.

## Purposes of This Book

This book will emphasize the absolute necessity of Christian function within the environment of freedom presently under siege by the political philosophy of progressivism. Many people, including many Christians, don't know what progressivism is, and many of the remaining don't really seem to care. The church adds to the problem of destroying personal freedom by burdening people with legalism. The book will associate the Christian way of life with a spiritual battle referred to as the angelic conflict. It will set Christianity in a dispensational perspective. It will place Christianity in perspective as a spiritual way of life to be lived "in the sphere of the Spirit" rather than a religious way of life dedicated to obedience to a set of ethical standards carried out in the energy of the flesh. It will cautiously provide new vocabulary with which to communicate biblical concepts. (It's the concept that's important, not the vocabulary term. Change the vocabulary if you must, but do not alter the concept to which it is attached.) It will provide the author's personal thoughts and understanding of the Christian way of life. Some of the terminology that he uses he has learned from various men and numerous sources over the years of his ministry. Please check the glossary for terms with which you may not be familiar.

## Target Groups

**Pastors.** This book will appeal to pastors whose desire it is to have a study guide to the spiritual side of the Christian way of life. They already know the "what." This will give them the missing "how."

**The Sick-and-Tired Church-goers.** This book will appeal to those who have become sick and tired of being sick and tired of going to church Sunday after Sunday with their unsolved problems in tow, being fed emotionalism or political correctness, and leaving church Sunday after Sunday with their unsolved problems still in tow. If these have never heard the "what," for certain they have never heard the "how." This book will give the both.

**The Church Dropouts.** This book will appeal to some who have already dropped-out of church, yet still believe that the truth is out there somewhere. The Holy Spirit will lead them to this book where they will find the truths that were missing in their traditional church experience. They've listened to the "what." They're looking for the "how."

**Certain Teenagers.** This book will appeal to certain teenagers who early in their lives have determined that there is something terribly wrong with this world and someone must have an answer. This book will point them in the right direction. It will give them hope and something upon which to build. This youngest generation is intelligent and will listen if someone will first love them with agape love, shoot-straight with them, and then demonstrate the life of Christ to them. They want to know the "what," and they'll be challenged by the "how."

**God knows.** This book will appeal to those being prepared by God through the circumstances of life. He knows who they are. He can lead them to this book that will lead them to Him.

# Read or Study?

In some places this book will need to be studied rather than read. The author understands that the book contains terminology that may be new to the reader, and he understands that there are sections that contain technical information such as Greek grammar that is presented to support his theses. If the technical side is too much for you, jump beyond it to the principles that it supports.

Here's a legitimate question that might be asked of this author. "Why do you think it's necessary to give us this kind of technical information that we don't really understand?" He says, "Great question." This technical information is not really for you. It's for those like the Judaizers who came in behind the Apostle Paul and tried to dissuade those who had heard the truth from Paul. Today's naysayers will say to you, "Where in the world did this man get that?" Well, he's setting forth in this book the "where did this man get that" so that you can point them to the technical data, and then point them on to him. Their argument is with this author, not you, and he'll answer their questions. You can rest assured that the Holy Spirit's confirmation in your human spirit of the truths in this book cannot be overcome by a naysayers "Where'd he get that?" They're really not looking for answers. Their desire is simply to divert you away from the truth. Don't let it happen.

# Concerning Terminology: Big Words, New Words

There may be big words and new words encountered in this book that will relate to the Christian way of life. You might again ask, "Why is there a need to use such big words or new words?" This, too, is a great question. For those Christians who are receiving some degree of Bible teaching today, it's generally shallow because of the five generation slide away from absolute truth. Christian terminology has lost its meaning or had its meaning distorted. Shallowness of thought has caused major biblical concepts to become lost to the church. To bring these concepts back into focus, we're going to have to dig deeper into God's Word to rediscover those deeper truths that will give solutions to the many complex problems that we face in today's world.

The State of Arkansas has the only diamond mine in the world open to the public. You're invited to prospect for diamonds. Can you imagine going to this diamond mine in Murfreesboro, Arkansas, with a little tin cup and a little tin shovel to scratch around in the earth's surface in an attempt to find a precious gem-a surface that has been scratched in by every prospector who has ever entered the grounds? Forget the little tin cup and little tin shovel. What we need is a backhoe to get down in deep where the really precious gems are.

In that same manner, to solve today's complex problems, we need more than another touchy-feely sermon or joining hands for another round of kum-ba-yah. We need to go to spiritual Murfreesboro, the Bible, with our spiritual backhoe, heart-hunger, and dig deeply enough to find those spiritual gems that are required to meet today's problems head-on! Your spiritual backhoe is your heart-hunger that will not stop digging and will not stop meditating until the truth is understood, believed, and applied. This book is your spiritual Murfreesboro. You alone know the level of your heart-hunger.

# A Sequel

This book is foundational for a sequel to follow that will focus on a deeper understanding of the old-man new-man concepts touched upon in this book and found primarily in the writings of the Apostle Paul.

# Acknowledgements

Over the years of my Christian life I have been influenced by many men who were involved in Christian ministry. It is my desire to acknowledge them. Acknowledgement does not imply that any of them agree with me theologically.

**John T. Goad.** John was the Southern Baptist navy chaplain under whose ministry my wife and I became born-again believers while I was stationed at the U.S. Naval Station, Trinidad, W.I., in 1962. Within a six month period of time, as well as I am able to remember, approximately 36 persons became born-again believers under John's ministry. I was 27 years old and had never heard the Gospel prior to meeting him. He presented a clear Gospel message from the pulpit in the navy chapel Sunday after Sunday. I came under the conviction of the Holy Spirit during a Sunday morning chapel service while singing in the chapel choir. I trusted Jesus Christ to be my Savior and received my so great eternal salvation. Three months later, under his ministry, I acknowledged my spiritual gift of Pastor-Teacher. The hours this man allowed me to spend with him for the eighteen months after I was saved is unbelievable. He mentored me from his pulpit, in his office, on the fishing peer into the early hours of the morning, in his car on the way to revival meetings all over the island. We never lost contact with one another. On October 15, 1999, I officiated his funeral.

**Emit O. Ray.** Emit was the first Southern Baptist missionary to the Island of Trinidad. John Goad introduced many of us from the naval station to Emit's ministry. Emit and John and I travelled together on many occasions to revival meetings around the island. I listened and learned as they talked about the Bible and the Christian way of life as we rode along together. Emit had a significant impact on my vision for foreign missions. The weekly Bible studies conducted under his home–it was built on stilts-helped to establish me in the faith before I left the navy in 1963.

**John R. Hagan.** John was my family's first Pastor after I left the navy. My wife and I met John and Lois Hagan in a Sunday School class at Broadman Baptist Church in Cuyahoga Falls, Ohio. John and Lois had been appointed as home missionaries to Akron, Ohio. They were there to establish the first Sothern Baptist Church in Akron. John and Lois mentored my wife and me from 1963-1968. It was through John and Lois that I came to understand the importance of home missions. We started as the Akron Baptist Chapel on Sundays in the rented Jewish War Veterans building, later becoming Central Baptist Church. John and Lois introduced us to associational meetings, state conventions, national conventions, home mission's week and foreign mission's week at Ridgecrest, North Carolina. It was through Lois that my wife and I came to appreciate the importance of preschool work in a local church. I became an ordained minister at First Baptist Church, England, Arkansas, under John's ministry in 1969. John introduced me to the prison ministry after he became the chaplain at Tucker Prison in Tucker, Arkansas.

**Robert B. Thieme, Jr.** I first heard of his ministry in 1965 after giving my personal testimony to a group of business men in Akron, Ohio. I was reintroduced to his ministry in 1969 by a lady friend of my family while I was in seminary in Fort Worth, Texas. I knew him as Colonel R.B. Thieme, Jr. and called him Colonel. It was through him that I learned to teach the Word of God by the ICE method: **I**sagogically, **C**ategorically, and **E**xegetically. I was reintroduced to him again in 1973 by Rev. W.O. Vaught, Pastor of Immanuel Baptist Church. I had become discouraged as a young pastor, and went to see Dr. Vaught at his church office. During that visit that lasted less than fifteen minutes, he gave me the following advice: "Get on Bob Thieme's tapes and stay there for five years." I went home, called Grace Tapes and Publications at Berachah Church in Houston, Texas, ordered my first set of four track, seven inch tapes and began transcribing the Colonel's recorded messages. I owe a considerable amount of my knowledge of Bible doctrine to this man. I received encouragement from other pastors to teach his concepts, but was encouraged by them to change the terminology that he used to identify the concepts that he taught. I refused to do so because I believed that there was no better way to say what needed to be said than through the terminology that I had learned from him. I continue to use much of his terminology for that same reason. There seems to be no better way to say it. Not only was he a great Bible teacher, but through personal encounters with him, I found him to be one of the most gracious men I have ever met.

**W.O. Vaught.** Dr. Vaught was the pastor of Immanuel Baptist Church in Little Rock, Arkansas. He is the man that I credit with introducing me to R.B. Thieme, Jr., in a meaningful way. Dr. Vaught and I remained personal friends until his death. During a personal encounter, he offered me his vast personal tape library, and said I would be its recipient before his death. He later called me and asked if he could retract his offer for two reasons. He knew that my collection of the Colonel's tapes was vast, and he had met another young pastor that he felt would benefit from his personal tape library. I consented, and this younger pastor became the recipient of Dr. Vaught's tapes. After he retired, he supplied my pulpit on several occasions at the independent, non-denominational Bible Doctrine Church of Little Rock (BDCLR). He preached his last sermon at BDCLR.

**Lewis Sperry Chafer.** I was given my first set of L.S. Chafer's eight volume Systematic Theology by Gin North in Forth Worth, Texas, in 1969. It was from this set of theology books that I seriously came to grips with dispensational theology. I have been privileged to teach through this set of theology books in a classroom setting on two separate occasions.

**Miles Stanford.** I was introduced to the writings of Stanford in 1970 while pastoring North Maple Baptist Church in Stuttgart, Arkansas. His booklets and website have served as resource material as I learned from him the concepts of Pauline Dispensationalism and the identification and reckoning truths of Romans 6. I had the privilege of talking with him personally by phone in the latter years of his life.

**Others Pastors Who Have Influenced My Ministry.** The following named men have influenced my Christian life even though they may not realize it. For this reason, I name them here: Dr. W.A. Criswell, Dr. Roy Fish, Rev. Herbert Hodges, Rev. Damon Shook, Rev. Ronald Condren, Rev. Johnny Jackson, and Dr. Gene Williams.

**Other Pastors and Friends Who Have Impacted My Ministry.** Adema, Ronald; Anderson, Darryl; Andoy, Federico; Ayop, Alex; Blackwood, Dub and Joyce; Cabilan, Gilbert; Cunningham, Gene; Dadula, Carlito; DeCastro, Luisito; Ellis, Steven; Eubanks, Michael; Garmon, Michael; Goetz, Dick; Horton, Gerald; Kendrick, Lemoyne and Bettye; Goad, Mark; Hiquiana, Dan; Johnson, Scott; Limjuco, Roger; Morrell, Richard; Pedres, Eser; Rosenblum, Al; Sejera, Nestor; Strickland, R.V; Udell, Eugene; Wells, Vernon; West, Brad; White, Theophilus; Williamson, Mark; Wynn, Ronald.

# Section 1

# Christianity and the Angelic Conflict

# Chapter 1

# The "Why" and "Where" Questions

There are several important "why" and "where" questions related to the angelic conflict. For example: Why did God the Father decree to create in the first place? Why did God decree the creation of man? Why does sin exist? Why does suffering exist? Where did we come from? Why are we here? Where are we going? All of these questions are related to the Christian way of life and the angelic conflict.

For the sake of discussion, let's assign the following: A="why and where questions;" B=the Christian way of life; C=angelic conflict; and let's assign the=sign to the phrase "is related to."

Now consider this. If A=B, and A=C, then B=C. Translated, this says that if the "why and the where questions" are related to the Christian way of life, and the "why and the where questions" are related to the angelic conflict, then the Christian way of life is related to the angelic conflict.

Here's the point. Christianity, as a way of life designed for us by the God of all creation, will not make much sense to anyone unless a relationship can be established among the why and where questions, the Christian way of life, and the angelic conflict. Let's establish the relationship.

## Why Did God the Father Decree to Create in the First Place?

This is a fair question in view of the horrific circumstances of life, such as, wars, rumors of wars, earthquakes, tsunamis, tornadoes, mudslides, divorce, rape, child abuse, murders, and kidnappings. Where do we stop? Some ask that if God knew in advance that events such as these were going to occur, then why did He create in the first place? When this question is sincerely asked, the answers often reflect biblical ignorance or extreme naïveté. "Well, He created because He was lonely." Oh, really? or

"He created because He needed someone to love." Oh, really? From where do answers like these come? They certainly don't come from the Bible.

Let's ask the question one more time. Why did God the Father decree creation in the first place? The biblical answer is that He decreed creation for the purpose of glorifying Himself through the manifestation of the unity of His attributes. His attributes: sovereignty, eternal life, love, justice, absolute righteousness, omnipotence, omniscience, omnipresence, immutability, and veracity. Every verse of Scripture that speaks of the glory of God addresses this issue.

The world might respond to this answer with the following comment: "Well, isn't that arrogant that God would want to glorify Himself?" No, it's not arrogant when absolute righteousness is understood to be His very nature. It's His absolute righteousness that brings His decrees into perspective. Anyone as intrinsically good as He is good is incapable of arrogance.

But what about the manifestation of the unity of His attributes? What does that mean? Be sure that what is true of the attributes of God the Father is also true of the attributes of God the Son and God the Holy Spirit. Here, though, the focus is only on God the Father because He is the Author of the plan to create everything. Consider the meaning of "the manifestation of the unity of His attributes?" Each attribute has its own intrinsic nature that reflects its own unique nature when manifested. Each attribute functions differently. No single attribute manifests itself in a manner similar to others. Each attribute has its own integrity that never waivers. When two or more attributes work together simultaneously, they manifest unity. They do not compete with one another for dominance. They work together harmoniously to manifest their inherent natures in unity. One attribute never has to lend assistance to another because of some inherent weakness or flaw. If the integrity of even one divine attribute ever slightly fails, then, the One who claims to be God is a fraud. He is not God, never was God, nor ever will be God. The good news is that His attributes will forever manifest themselves in unity.

So, why did God the Father decree creation in the first place? He did so to glorify Himself through the manifestation of the unity of His attributes.

# Why Did God the Father Decree the Creation of Man?

God the Father decreed the creation of man to resolve the spiritual battle referred to by some as the angelic conflict. A fair and honest question might be asked. How could man possibly assist God in resolving a battle between Himself and angels?

The Bible states that man was created lower than the angels (Hebrews 2:7). This indicates that angels were created higher than man. From the moment of their creation, angels were required to be obedient to their Creator if they wanted to retain relationship and fellowship with Him. Some chose disobedience and lost both fellowship and relationship with their Creator. God offered the fallen angels a plan of salvation. (Hebrews 2:2). They rejected His offer. He, then, sentenced them to the lake of fire. Satan objected and appealed his sentence. So, God, in fairness to Satan, created man to resolve the issue. Man was created lower than the angels, and was required to be obedient. Here's God's reasoning. If man created lower than the angels would manifest obedience, the issue is that the higher creature could have, but wasn't, and God would be justified in carrying out His sentence. At the end of human history, every objection raised by Satan will have been satisfactorily answered by man's obedience, and Satan and the fallen angels will be sent to the lake of fire as a consequence for rejecting God the Father's plan of angelic salvation.

Why, then, did God the Father decree the creation of man? He decreed the creation of man to assist in the resolution of the angelic conflict, and that's precisely why man is here on earth.

## Why Does Sin Exist?

To answer this question it seems reasonable to assume that a creator is of higher order than that which he creates. Applying this to God and creation, Creator God is of higher order than anything that He creates. Therefore, if obedience is required from One or the other, the Creator or the created, it reasonable to conclude that the lower should be obedient to the Higher. Thus, Satan and man as created beings are required to be obedient to whatever guidelines were established for them by the One who created them.

Satan failed and man failed. Their failure is called sin. So, from whence came sin? It first occurred in heaven, in the throne room of God, when Satan's disobedience was manifested in the form of "five I wills" recorded in Isaiah 14:13-14. Man's disobedience is recorded for us in Genesis 3:6. So, when the question is asked, "Why sin?" the answer is because God's creatures acted in disobedience to divinely established standards-first, in heaven by Satan and the fallen angels, and then on earth by Adam and Eve. God did not create sin. He created creatures with volition that gave them capacity to rebel. Sin is manufactured by an act of volition manifested toward a divine prohibition.

Sin came into existence among the creatures of God, both angelic and human, because they chose to function contrary to His will for their lives; and sin exists within the human race today for exactly the same reason.

# Why Does Suffering Exist?

Suffering entered human history when man fell in the Garden of Eden. Suffering is the decreed consequence of disobedience toward the will of God. Man became disobedient. Enter suffering. Suffering can be mental, emotional, or physical in nature.

There was no suffering in the Garden of Eden prior to the moral fall of Adam and Eve. They were living in perfect environment in perfect harmony with the God who created them. No suffering there! However, with their moral fall, Adam and Eve lost their relationship with God and suffering entered the picture. It would be erroneous to conclude that if suffering resulted from a broken relationship with God, suffering would disappear if the relationship were reestablished. Not quite so. With the moral fall of man in the Garden of Eden, we understand that all of creation fell with man. Man suffers and all of creation suffers with him (Romans 8:22). Suffering is man's lot until the end of human history. At that time God will fulfill His decree to destroy the present heaven and present earth. He will then create a new heaven and a new earth in which and upon which suffering will be non-existent. Suffering will remain the eternal lot of every fallen angel and every human being whose eternal residence is the lake of fire. There is no suffering to compare with eternal separation from the living God who Authored the creation of everything.

Suffering is the decreed consequence of disobedience toward the will of God.

# Where Did We Come From?

Our ancestors were not fish who came from the sea, nor were they monkeys who swung from a tree. Our ancestry makes its way back to Adam and Eve who were created in the Garden of Eden by an eternally existing God. The theory of evolution is just that, a theory, and an old-man theory at that. The theory of evolution rejects the notion of fiat creation. Jesus Christ. the $2^{nd}$ Person of the Godhead spoke, and there he was. The visible part of Adam was formed from the dust of the earth, but the invisible part of Adam was created from nothing when God breathed into his nostrils the "breath of lives"-not life singular, but lives plural, namely, soul life and spiritual life.

Human beings did not evolve. They were spoken into existence by Jesus Christ.

# Why Are We Here?

"We" is a reference to mankind, and mankind is "here" on this planet to resolve the spiritual battle referred to as the angelic conflict. The conflict is resolved by acts of obedience to the rules for living relative to the dispensation in which man lives. The Age of the Gentiles required man to be obedient to rules associated with Inherent Law. The Age of Israel required man to be obedient to rules associated with Mosaic Law. The Church Age requires man to be obedient to rules associated with Grace. The Age of Christ, the millennium, will require man to be obedient to rules associated with Kingdom Law.

A common misconception in Christendom is that biblical rules have no dispensational distinctions. Rules for living contained in Inherent Law, Mosaic Law, Grace, and Kingdom Law are viewed as common for all mankind throughout human history. It is conceded that there may be a similarity of rules from one dispensation to the next; however, it is their dissimilarity from one dispensation to the next that makes the rules in one dispensation uniquely different from another. The fact that similarity exists does not imply that a human being is responsible to the authority of a different dispensation simply because similar rules exist. Let's consider an example:

- Marriage: a principle associated with the Age of the Gentiles, Age of Israel, and the Church Age.
- Tithing: the concept of tithing is found in the Age of the Gentiles and again under the Mosaic Law.

    Question: Since there is a similar principle of marriage in the Age of the Gentiles, the Age of Israel, and the Church Age, and tithing occurred in both the Age of the Gentiles and the

Age of Israel, should a Christian feel obligated to tithe based on a similarity of marriage and tithing practices in the Age of the Gentiles and the Age of Israel?

Answer: The Christian is under no obligation to tithe. The principle of giving in the Church Age is "grace giving." In the Church Age, the amount to be given is determined by Holy Spirit leadership, not by a certain percentage prescribed for a previous dispensation.

Since I live in the Church Age and follow Church Age rules similar to rules in other dispensations of time, because of similarity, why should I conclude that I am responsible to be obedient to Inherent Law, Mosaic Law, or Kingdom Law? The truth is that I'm not and you're not either! And until we understand why we are here on this planet, the reason being to resolve the angelic conflict through obedience to the rules established for our dispensation, the concept of dispensational distinctions will mean nothing to anyone but the hungry heart. Are you hungry enough to stop and listen?

Human beings are on this earth to resolve the angelic conflict by obedience to the rules for living associated with their respective dispensation.

# Where Are We Going?

This question refers to final destinations of which there are three: the new heaven, the new earth, and the lake of fire. Hell is not mentioned here because it's not a final destination. Going to hell is like going to the county jail awaiting transfer to the state penitentiary. Man goes to hell awaiting transfer to the lake of fire at the end of human history.

The new heaven is the final destination of born-again Jews and Gentiles who become saved only during the Church Age. The new earth is the destination of Gentiles and Jews saved during all other dispensational periods-the Age of the Gentiles, the Age of Israel, the Tribulation which is the final seven years of the Age of Israel, and the Age of Christ (the millennium).

The lake of fire is the final destination of all human beings who die having rejected Jesus Christ as Savior throughout their entire lifetime. While many people speak of God *sending* people to hell or the lake of fire, He does so only in the sense that hell and the lake of fire are the decreed consequential destinies of those who reject Jesus Christ as Savior for an entire lifetime.

The concept of *sending* someone to hell or the lake of fire may be perceived as divinely malicious or an act of an angry God, a God of no mercy or love. Quite the contrary. When the word *sending* is understood to be associated with a decree established in eternity past, maliciousness, anger, and lack of mercy and love are removed from the equation. In fact, it establishes God as the Gentleman that He is, demonstrating nothing but respect-that's agape love-for the decisions of every human being, including the decision to reject Jesus Christ as Savior during one's entire lifetime. God the Father decreed in eternity past, that throughout human history, man would be used to resolve the angelic conflict. He also decreed that if man freely and willfully chooses to reject Jesus Christ as Savior throughout his entire lifetime, he would by default be accepting the consequence of an eternal destiny in the lake of fire. Man chooses his destiny-the new heaven, the new earth, or the lake of fire.

There are three final destinations: the new heaven for born-again Christians, the new earth for Jews and Gentiles from dispensations other than the Church Age, and the lake of fire for unbelievers in every dispensation.

# Chapter 2

# Asking the Right Question

Christians are fighting a very real spiritual battle on three fronts: the world, the flesh, and the devil. Most Christians have no trouble identifying the works-of-the-flesh and recognize them as repugnant to God. They also recognize the work of Satan to be equally repugnant to God. It's the world that poses the problem.

We have heard of the world, but recognizing it when participating in it seems elusive. If questioned about sinful activity, the Christian says, "You're right. This is sinful, and it's wrong." If questioned about something they believe, they might say, "You're right. That's false doctrine, and my thinking is wrong." However, if questioned about decisions that identify them with the world, they might say, "Well, what's wrong with it?" No. The question is not what's wrong with it? The question is what's right with it, and the answer is simple. There's NOTHING right with it.

Generally speaking, sinful activity is not difficult to identify. Sins are listed in the Bible, and when your thinking, your speech, or your actions match something in the list, you realize that you're guilty of sin. The believer who identifies himself with the devil realizes that he has done so because he has accepted a false doctrine and considered that false doctrine to be truth.

However, there seems to be a subtleness attached to identifying worldliness in our Christian lives, and yet the 1 John 2:15 is very clear:

> "Love not the world, neither the things that are in the world. If any man love the world, the love of the Father is not in him." (KJV)

We are told to love not the world or the things in it. Yet, when someone who identifies worldly activity in another Christian's life and questions the worldly Christian about his or her activity, the worldly Christian generally responds by asking, "Well, what's wrong with it?" This response is a manifestation of spiritual naïveté at best and spiritual ignorance at worst.

The thing that makes worldliness so difficult for many to identify is that it involves common things of everyday life, such as, family, marriage, friendships, material things, career, money, education, health, vacations, retirement, the arts, government, law-just to name a few. How could any of this be considered wrong? Family wrong? Marriage wrong? Friendships wrong? Material things wrong? Career wrong? Money wrong? Education wrong? Health wrong? Vacations wrong? Retirement wrong? Arts wrong? Government wrong? Law wrong?

Wait a minute, preacher. What's wrong with these things? Well, that's a fair question, but it begs-the-question. The question that should be asked is not what's wrong with these things? The question that should be asked is what's right with them? To ask, "What's wrong with them?" implies that nothing is wrong with them, and that implication is spiritually dangerous.

Sinful activity is intrinsically offensive to God. False doctrine is intrinsically offensive to God; but when you are talking about such things as family, marriage, friendships, material things, career, money, education, health, vacations, retirement, the arts, government, or law, man's fundamental thought is that if these things bring pleasure, happiness, and joy to one's life, how could you possibly ask anything other than what's wrong with them?

The problem associated with family, marriage, friendships, material things, career, money, education, health, vacations, retirement, the arts, government, or law is one of priority. Priority #1 in the Christian life is the goal of becoming like Christ in His humanity-a very reachable goal. The means of reaching that goal is Christian function from the source the new-man. However, if pursuit in any worldly area takes precedence over becoming like Christ, that pursuit is a manifestation of maladjusted priority.

So, what's wrong with family, marriage, friendships, material things, career, money, education, health, vacations, retirement, the arts, government, or law? The answer is nothing just as long as they don't take precedence over the Christian's pursuit of Christ-likeness.

So, what's wrong with family, marriage, friendships, material things, career, money, education, health, vacations, retirement, the arts, government, or law? The answer is everything if they take precedence over the Christian's pursuit of Christ-likeness.

Do not allow the world to fool you. We are told, "Love not the world, neither the things that are in the world." Look at that verse closely. Isn't it clear that Christians are told what not to do without a single word about how not to do it. I call this the "what" without the "how." How, then, do we love not he world? When the Christian finds it necessary to involve himself in the world or with things of the world, he honors God through obedience to this command by not allowing the use of the worldly thing to be prioritized higher than the priority that he assigns to his pursuit of Christ-likeness.

The Christian who does not understand the biblical concepts of old-man new-man, or how to live his life from the source of his new-man, defaults to old-man function. The net result is that while he may find the flesh and the devil repugnant, he may be lured into worldly activity by the world's pleasures because they are NOT intrinsically sinful. This causes him to make the statement, "What's wrong with it?" This is the wrong question. The real question remains, "What's RIGHT with it?"

Priority is the issue when involved with the world and the things of the world. Priority makes the difference between what's wrong with it and what's right with it. Priority makes the difference between spiritual disaster and momentum into a Christ-like life. Are you asking others what's wrong with it or are you asking them what's right with it? Your understanding will determine which question you ask.

# Section 2

# What Is Christianity?

# Chapter 3

# Christianity and the Big Picture

The "big picture" of human history is the angelic conflict. It's the backdrop against which all of human life is lived; yet, it's one of the most neglected, abused, and least understood concepts found in the Word of God. The liberal side of Christianity neglects it, and the Pentecostal and Charismatic world abuse it. If you tell some on the liberal side of Christianity that the Bible teaches that angels married woman from among the human race, had sexual relationships with them, and bore them children, they look at you like you've lost your mind. When you listen to the Pentecostal and Charismatic world, the devil made them do it. He's whispering in their ears; he's planting thoughts in their heads; he's controlling people's lives; and he's inflicting people with disease-none of which is true.

    Until the angelic conflict is properly understood, life will make no sense when trying to explain its disasters and catastrophes. Until it is properly understood, it seems absurd to tell someone that God requires the Christian to achieve and retain experiential victory over the world, the flesh, and the devil. Actually, it's a knowledge of the angelic conflict that puts all of life's events into perspective. Therefore, a summary of the angelic conflict is in order so as to bring all of life into perspective with God's Holy Word.

# Putting Life into Biblical Perspective

    The Christian Godhead comprises three Persons who have always existed. There has never been a time when They didn't exist. Prior to the development of a plan to create anything, the Godhead would have been known as the 1$^{st}$, 2$^{nd}$, and 3$^{rd}$ Persons of the Godhead. The concept of Father, Son, and Holy Spirit was potential, residing in the omniscience of the three Persons of the Godhead. The concept of Father, Son, and Holy Spirit did not become a reality until the plan designed by the 1$^{st}$ Person was accepted by the 2$^{nd}$ and 3$^{rd}$ Persons. This occurred during a meeting in eternity past. It was attended by the three Persons of the Godhead and is addressed in Acts 2:23. The meeting is noted by the underlined portion of the following verses.

> Acts 2:23 Him, being delivered by <u>the determinate counsel</u> and foreknowledge of God, ye have taken, and by wicked hands have crucified and slain: (KJV)
>
> Acts 2:23 this *Man,* delivered over by <u>the predetermined plan</u> and foreknowledge of God, you nailed to a cross by the hands of godless men and put *Him* to death. (NASB)
>
> Acts 2:23 This man was handed over to you by <u>God's set purpose</u> and foreknowledge; and you, with the help of wicked men, put him to death by nailing him to the cross. (NIV)

During this meeting, the 1st Person of the Godhead, now known as God the Father, disclosed His position as the author of a plan to create. The 2nd Person of the Godhead, now known as God the Son, accepted His position as the executor of the plan. The 3rd Person of the Godhead, now referred to as the Holy Spirit, accepted His role as the revealer and restorer to the plan.

In the first act of creation, Jesus Christ created angels (Job 38:4-7). He later created the universe. Note by the underline in this verse that the angels were present when the earth was created.

> Job 38:4 "Where were you when I laid the foundations of the earth? Tell me, if you know so much. 5 Do you know how its dimensions were determined and who did the surveying? 6 What supports its foundations, and who laid its cornerstone 7 as the morning stars sang together <u>and all the angels shouted for joy</u>? (NLT)

Let's consider a chronology of historical events.

> Jesus Christ created angels.
> Lucifer (Satan) served as a ceremonial guard of the throne of Jesus Christ. (Ezekiel 28:14)
> Eventually, Lucifer (Satan) sinned. (Isaiah 14:13-14)
> One-third of the angels followed after Satan. (Revelation 12:4)
> God the Father offered the fallen angels a plan of salvation. (Hebrews 2:2)

The fallen angels rejected the offer of salvation.
The fallen angels were found guilty.
God the Father sentenced fallen angels to the lake of fire. (Matthew 25:41)
Satan appealed his sentence (an inductive conclusion paraphrased). "How can a loving God possibly send one of His creatures to the lake of fire?" God said, "Stick around a minute and I'll show you."
God the Father ordered the creation of man to resolve the spiritual battle referred to as the angelic conflict.
God the Father decreed the creation of man to be lower than the angels. (Hebrews 2:7) He reasoned that if the lower creature will be obedient, the higher creature could have been, but wasn't, and He will have vindicated Himself for sentencing Satan to the lake of fire. The lake of fire is not a place of punishment. It is the consequential location for rejecting a redemptive condition. Let's expand that idea.

God the Father is just (fair) by nature. This raises a question. How fair would He be under the following conditions? Suppose that He offered the fallen angels a plan of redemption with the benefit of heaven as their eternal abode if they would only accept His redemptive proposal. Further suppose that God the Father determined that heaven would be the eternal abode of the fallen angels even if they would reject His redemptive plan. Under these conditions, the fallen angels would cry out, "Foul! You've violated your own essence. You're totally unfair because you've offered us the same eternal residence no matter how we choose. What if it's our desire to be eternally separated from You, and You have denied us that alternative? Even if we should choose to reject Your redemptive plan, we're locked into Your eternal presence." The fallen angels would be right. God would be totally unfair and that contradicts His essence; therefore, if He offers them a plan of redemption with the benefit of heaven as their eternal abode, He must decree an alternate eternal residence should they freely determine to reject His redemptive offer. As a matter of justice, God the Father decreed the lake of fire as the alternative to heaven for those fallen angels who by their own free-will would reject His redemptive offer. Now, the fallen angels have no argument with the justice of God.

As a final thought, the lake of fire should not be considered a place of punishment designed by God to torment His creatures throughout eternity future. Using His own sovereignty, He simply decreed an alternate eternal location that will be devoid of every form of divine presence. By divine design, sovereignty limited omnipresence in this matter. Therein lays the torment, the torturous nature of the lake of fire, a location eternally devoid of divine presence. It's just the opposite of heaven and the new earth. It's the difference between the eternal presence of God and the eternal absence of God. How can anything be considered punishment if by divine design, the very nature of divine justice demands an alternate location for those who personally make a choice, the consequence of which is completely understood before it is made. The fallen angels knew in advance the very nature of their destiny if they rejected God's redemptive offer-eternal separation from the God who created them. The eternal torture of the lake of fire is not the fire. It's the absence of the presence of God that will torment fallen creatures throughout all of eternity future. When this is understood, it's only a small step away from concluding that the lake of fire is figurative language that the finite mind can understand when God the Father is trying to explain and make clear the very nature of the consequence of rejecting His redemptive plan—eternal separation from the God of all creation. That's torture-but one of choice!

Luke 16:23 describes hell as torments. "Torments" does not imply punishment. It implies the decreed nature of a location to which an unbeliever has chosen to go by virtue of a willful decision to reject God the Father's redemptive plan of salvation. Like the lake of fire, the absence of the presence of God is what creates the torments of hell.

Now, let's return to the chronology.

> Human history is the arena for the appeal phase of Satan's trial.
> Human history is divided into four dispensations with a separate set of rules to guide the people living in each dispensation: Age of the Gentiles: Inherent Law; Age of Israel, Mosaic Law; Church Age: Grace; and the Age of Christ (millennium) Kingdom Law.
> Each dispensation represents a specific phase of Satan's appeal trial.
> God the Father planned for mankind to serve as witnesses for the Prosecution.

As believers serve God in each dispensation, the question arises as to the sufficiency of God's grace during that dispensation. When a believer serves God obediently according to the rules for his dispensation, certain objections that Satan raised about the fairness of his sentence are answered by that believer.

Note that in the Age of the Gentiles and the Age of Israel, obedience to Inherent Law and the Mosaic Law was carried out in the energy of the flesh; but during the Church Age, God the Father has raised the standard. The standard is not some form of Law, but a "walk within the sphere of the Spirit." As a result of a five generation slide away from the absolute truths of God's Holy Word, Christianity has degenerated into a religion that requires obedience to its ethical standards from the energy of the flesh. That's tantamount to living the Christian way of life from the source of the old-man under another form of law. It's not until the Christian way of life is carried out from the source of the new-man that believers will favorably impact the resolution of the angelic conflict in the Church Age. The Christian way of life is no different from previous dispensations in that God demands obedience; however, in the Church Age, He demands obedience from the source of the new-man. This means doing the right thing (that's obedience) in the RIGHT WAY (that's obedience from the source of the new-man).

Here's the problem. In liberal Christian circles, the old-man new-man concepts are rarely if ever taught. In fundamental circles, they may never be mentioned, and if they are, more often than not they are taught incorrectly. For example, there's the second-blessing experience. Some say that after you've received it, you've been experientially sanctified so as to have eradicated the sinful nature from your life. These people have a difficult time convincingly explaining their personal sins after they receive the so-called second blessing. Yet, there are others who have been spiritually blinded by their own paradigm based upon a faulty exegesis that has led them to dismiss the possibility of any victory over the sinful nature. You hear such things as, "We all HAVE TO sin," or "We ALL sin every day," or some such statement that is born out of ignorance or rejection of truth.

By the time human history reaches the seven year Tribulation period, every objection raised by Satan will have been so sufficiently answered by Christians during the Church Age, and believers during the two previous dispensations, that the only thing Satan will have left in rebuttal is violence, and that's why the Tribulation period will be the most violent period of human history known to man.

# Summary and Conclusion

The "big picture" of life requires a thorough understanding of the angelic conflict because it's the angelic conflict that clarifies the otherwise unresolved "why's" of life. Why this? Why that? Why something else? Why should I as a Christian be required by God the Father to get victory over my sinful nature so as to have ignorance as my only legitimate excuse for sinning mentally, verbally, or overtly? The answer is simple when you understand the angelic conflict. Human history is the appeal phase of Satan's trial, and God the Father has set the standard for Christian living so far above fleshly reach that only by appropriating the sufficient provision of His grace can the Christian fulfill God's plan for his life so as to be worthy enough to be called to the witness stand during Satan's appeal trial. "Witness, take the stand," God the Father calls out. "No, not me Lord. You know I've failed to reach Your standard," the Christian cries out. "Yes, that one God; I dare you to call that one," Satan responds. God's reply, "Well, that's right. Better skip that one. You'll destroy that one on the witness stand. Let's see. Let me look around. Oh, yeah. There's the one I want. Witness, take the stand!" God has found a Christian who by acts of his or her own volition has freely chosen to fulfill the plan of God for his or her life and is able to testify during Satan's appeal trial to the sufficiency of God's grace under all conditions of life. On the witness stand, this Christian is able to testify that God the Father's plan sufficiently provided all that was necessary to obediently reach the standard of Christ-likeness in the right way-obedience to the ethical standards of the Christian way of life while functioning from the source of the new-man. Doing the right thing-that's obedience-is not enough. It's obedience done in the right way, namely, from the source of the new-man. This is why it's imperative that every Christian understand the HOW-TO in the Christian way of life-"Operation KRRY." Whatever Satan's objections were regarding his condemnation to the lake of fire in eternity past, his objections were radical enough that God the Father requires Church Age believers to match the character of His Son's humanity so as to be qualified as witnesses during the Church Age phase of Satan's appeal trial.

WITNESS, TAKE THE STAND!!
Could that witness be you?

# Chapter 4

# Christianity in Historical Perspective

Religion can be defined as man by man's efforts trying to gain the approval of God. However, Christianity is not a religion. Christianity is a spiritual way of life that begins with a personal relationship with Jesus Christ, the relationship established by faith-alone in Christ-alone. Christianity, as a way of life, is dispensationally associated with the Church Age. Prior to the Church Age there were no born-again Christians on earth in physical bodies. After the rapture of the Church, there will be no born-again Christians on earth in physical bodies.

Let's view Christianity another way. Christianity is eternal in nature. Christianity has always been. There has never been a time when Christianity wasn't. Christianity extends from eternity past into eternity future. How is this possible?

Christianity is eternal in nature only in the sense that it existed, exists, and will exist in the omniscience of all three Persons of the Christian Godhead. However, insofar as its historical existence is concerned, Christianity as a divinely designed way of life did not come into existence experientially until after the resurrection, ascension, and session of Jesus Christ at the right hand of God the Father.

If Christianity is to be understood as a *spiritual* way of life, it will help to understand some divinely ordained chronologies.

## The Order of Creations Viewed Chronologically

Everything created was not created simultaneously. There were separate acts of creation with a gap of time between each act of creation. The elapsed time between each creative act is unknown to man. The order of creations follows: first, the creation of angels; second, the creation of the universe; third, the creation of animal life and sea life; and finally, the creation of man.

## Dispensations Viewed Chronologically

There are four Dispensations related to human history: the Age of the Gentiles, the Age of Israel, the Church Age, and the Age of Christ (the millennium).

## Expanding the Chronology

An abridged expansion of chronology looks like this: the existence of the Triune Godhead, the creation of angels, the creation of the universe, the fall of angels, the judgment of angels, the creation of animals and sea life, the creation of man, the fall of man, the Dispensation of the Gentiles, the Dispensation of Israel, the Dispensation of the Church, the rapture of the Church, the bema seat judgment and the Tribulation occurring simultaneously, the Dispensation of Christ (the millennium), the great white throne judgment, and eternity future.

## Where Does Christianity Fit In?

Christianity is associated with the Church Age, and on a time line, the Church Age is perhaps a minimum of 4,000 years beyond the banishment of Adam and Eve from the Garden of Eden. This considered, it is fair to ask the question, "What, then, makes Christianity so important in the grand scheme of things?" The answer will only make sense when the real purpose for human history is correctly understood.

## The Real Purpose for Human History

God the Father is the Judge in heaven's courtroom. Satan is the defendant. Because Satan fell morally in eternity past, God the Father sentenced him and the angels who followed after him to the lake of fire. God the Father's attribute of justice required Him to permit Satan to appeal his sentence to the lake of fire. God the Father determined to create human beings to assist in the resolution of the angelic conflict. Since Satan was sentenced to the lake of fire in eternity past and will not be cast into the lake of fire until the end of human history, it seems fair to ask why the expanse of time between the sentence occurring in eternity past and the execution of that sentence at the end of human history? If Satan was found guilty in eternity past, why didn't God send him to go to the lake of fire before He created man?

Every time something horrible happens in life, some accuse Satan as being the *direct* cause. If that were so, and God the Father is omniscient, why in the world didn't He send Satan to go to the lake of fire in eternity past and save the human race all the heartache that is attributed to Satan? The answer is concluded inductively. Human history is the appeal phase of Satan's trial during which time God the Father has permitted Satan certain leeway to deal with human beings as they serve as God's witnesses in the appeal trial.

Human history is divided into dispensations of time, each dispensation representing a different phase of Satan's appeal trial. During each time period certain objections raised by Satan are answered by humans under the conditions prescribed by God for their respective dispensation. The Church Age is one of those dispensations, and Christianity is related to the Church Age.

## The Christian Way of Life During the Church Age

Assume for a moment that the concept of Church is related to the Church Age and that Christians are related to the Church. This means that Christians are related to the Church Age. All Christians do not agree on when the Church actually began. Some say in Abraham's tent. Some say with John the Baptist. Some say with Christ. Some say the Day of Pentecost AD 30. Some say with the Apostle Paul. Some say at the end of the Book of Acts. These differing points of view alter the manner in which the Christian way of life is perceived to be lived. Is it under some form of law or is it by grace? If Christians are confused about their own way of life, it's no wonder the world questions the relevance of Christianity in the grand scheme things. Before you tell someone what YOU believe is relevant, perhaps you should go back to the "So What?" chapter. The world is going to tell you that your understanding is just one opinion among many, none of which make much sense. Remember, you're talking to the world. Tragic, isn't it?

Well, there is a solution to this relevance issue, and the solution is subjective in nature. The issue is not whether you'll be able to convince others of the relevance of the Christian way of life in the grand scheme of things. The issue is whether YOU personally are convinced whether anyone else is or not. What is this convincing subjective way?

This convincing subjective way is the Holy Spirit bearing witness with YOUR human spirit (Romans 8:16). His roles of revealer and restorer to God the Father's plan are crucial in the life of every born-again Christian. He is responsible to bear witness with the human spirit of every believer who has positioned himself spiritually to receive communication from Him. You are positioned correctly when you meet the following preconditions simultaneously: born-again (John 3:3), clean before the Lord through confession of post-salvation sins (1 John 1:9), and wanting to want the will of God for your life (Philippians 2:13). Then, and only then, while functioning simultaneously in each of these preconditions, can the born-again Christian be absolutely certain of the Holy Spirit's witness within his human spirit.

Why is this method referred to as subjective? It's because the Holy Spirit's witness occurs inside the believer, not outside, but within the human spirit. People can argue with you until Jesus comes about this "subjective thing," as though you're telling them that you have some special means of correctly interpreting God's plan for the human race. Well, hello! That's exactly what you're telling them because the inspired, inerrant, infallible Word of God tells you that this is the way God operates, and you have proven God to be true by meeting the conditions necessary to receive your confirmation. Does your confirmation convince anyone else? No. Emphatically, NO! Confirmation is personal and private, and there is no confirmation for anyone who has not met the conditions for receiving this type of communication.

Caution! Beware! The following old-man logic will be levied against you. "Well, I've been told about this subjective thing by other Christians, and what claims to have been received by one contradicts what is said to have been received by another. As a result, I'm not going to believe what anyone tells me about some subjective means of receiving communication from God."

Here's the problem with that statement. It may be a valid observation, but it's an invalid conclusion. First of all, one Christian offering information received subjectively might have been right while the other was wrong. Second, many years ago in a college philosophy class in which I was enrolled, the professor made the following statement: "All swans are white until you see a black one." The fallacy of the specific argument posed by the person observing two Christians with contradictory evidence can fall under the all swans are white principle. Suppose both Christians were wrong. This is the "all swans are white" portion of the principle. Just because two Christians provide contradictory evidence does not mean that someone might not come along with evidence that lines up with God's Word. This is the "black swan" portion of the principle. The "black swan" is out there somewhere, but it won't be recognized until the antagonist gets right with God and follows the procedure required to receive this subjective confirmation. Science will especially argue against this; however, that doesn't make science right! As an aside, isn't it interesting that science doesn't discover scientific laws. It simply discovers the faithfulness of God.

Hhhhmmmm???? Just how important is it, then, that God has told the Christian that he is to walk by means of the Spirit? WOW! Christianity, in perspective, is not a religion by which its converts function in strict obedience to a set of rules. Christianity provides a set of guidelines to be followed while walking "in the sphere of the Spirit." Christianity is not a fleshly walk, but a walk by means of the Spirit that serves to resolve a portion of the angelic conflict. God the Father might be asking, "How are you walking?

# Chapter 5

# Christianity and Its Goal

Before we consider "Operation KRRY," we must consider the goal of the Christian way of life because "Operation KRRY" is the means by which the goal will be reached. What then is the ultimate goal of the Christian life?

Have you ever wondered how many times God has to say something before it should be considered true? It shouldn't take long to realize that if God is truth, and He is, then He only has to speak one time for us to know the truth that He is conveying.

Have you ever wondered if God has to speak only one time to convey truth, why He says the same thing more than once, even though He may say the same thing in slightly different ways? Some have conjectured humorously that God thinks that if He says the same thing more than once and in slightly different ways, maybe we as human being will finally "get-it." Well, here's one of those things that God says more than once, but in slightly different ways.

**The goal of the Christian life is to become exactly like Jesus Christ in His humanity.**

However, lest we spend our time looking at Jesus in the Gospels where He is featured performing supernatural after supernatural, we need to advance to the post-canon period of the Church Age where we should view Him as He would manifest Himself during this period of the angelic conflict. The perception that Jesus is "the same yesterday, today, and forever" and thereby passes on to you and me His supernatural works based upon Hebrews 13:8 is a false and misleading perception. Yes, He remains the same yesterday, today, and forever, but in essence only. His character never changes, but His works do. The old-man in every one of us favors the supernatural, while abhorring the sufferings that attend Christ-likeness in the devil's world. Seek the character of Christ, not the miracles that He performed. Please understand that when the goal of the Christian life is expressed as becoming like Christ in His humanity, it will always be expressed in the sense of Jesus manifesting Himself in the post-canon period of the Church Age, that is, focusing on His character, minus the miraculous.

Let's look at five different verses: Romans 8:29, Galatians 2:20, Galatians 4:19, 2 Corinthians 3:18, and Philippians 1:19. In these verses, God is conveying the same thought, but in different ways, namely, that the goal for every Christian is to become exactly like Christ in His humanity.

A word of caution is in order here. Each of the following verses will tell the Christian WHAT to do, but the HOW is missing. Keep this in mind as you study these verses. They express the WHAT without the HOW. The HOW will follow in a later chapter.

> **Romans 8:29** For whom he did foreknow, he also did predestinate *to be* **conformed to the image of his Son**, that he might be the firstborn among many brethren. (KJV)

**For whom he did foreknow.** "he," though not capitalized, is a reference to God the Father, the author of the divine plan for the human race that resolves the angelic conflict. The word "whom" refers to every born-again believer in the dispensation of the Church Age. The word "foreknow" is a reference to God the Father's omniscience looking forward from eternity past and knowing specifically who would place their faith-alone in Christ-alone to become the recipient of His so great salvation. It must be understood that God the Father's foreknowledge does not force anyone to believe. It simply recognizes beforehand what would eventually become so.

**he also did predestinate.** Again, "he" is God the Father, the author of the plan. "Predestinate" means to determine something ahead of time and takes us back to eternity past. The Father determined in eternity past that if anyone living in the Church Age would place their faith-alone in Christ-alone, a specific goal would already have been established for that Christian to reach. That goal is stated later in this verse. One thing needs to be certain. Predestinate does not mean to establish one's destiny in advance where that destiny is said to be heaven or hell. That concept is an old-man perversion of truth.

**to be conformed to the image of his Son.** THIS is the predetermined goal. God the Father determined in eternity past that the specific goal to be reached by every born-again believer in the Church Age is "to be conformed to the image of his Son." The word "conformed" refers to an outer expression of an inner nature. The word "image" refers to a likeness that is the result of a transforming process. In other words, becoming like Christ in His humanity is not accidental. You don't just stumble into it. This non-stumbling, non-accidental process leading the believer into the likeness of Christ's humanity is referred to as a "derived likeness"-the meaning of the word "image." The non-capitalized "his" refers to God the Father, and "Son" refers to Jesus Christ.

**that he might be the firstborn.** "he" refers to Jesus in His humanity. "firstborn" refers to Jesus, born physically the Son of God the Father, and born into the place of preeminence.

**among many brethren.** This refers to those who would later become sons of God through spiritual birth during the Church Age. If you are a born-again believer, this refers to you.

The image into which the Church Age believer is to be conformed is not visible in the believer at the moment of salvation, but becomes increasingly visible as spiritual growth takes place in the believer's life.
The following four verses point to the same goal to be reached in every Christian's life, namely, becoming like Christ in His humanity. For this reason, only the underlined portion of the verses will be considered.

> **Galatians 2:20** I am crucified with Christ: nevertheless I live; yet not I, but **Christ liveth in me**: and the life which I now live in the flesh I live by the faith of the Son of God, who loved me, and gave himself for me. (KJV)

The Apostle Paul states "Christ liveth in me." Paul was not speaking of himself as a brand new believer, but as a mature believer having moved through the process of transformation from an "I-centered" life into a "Christocentric" life. This process is also known as "experiential sanctification." Paul has grown to the point in his spiritual life that his thoughts, his feelings, his speech, his overt actions, and his rationales are the expressions of the very image of the humanity of Jesus Christ. Although Jesus Christ was seated at the right hand of God the Father in heaven at the time Paul was writing this verse, Paul's lifestyle was reflecting the very life of Jesus Christ as though He were present on earth. If you had been able to see Paul, his physical appearance wouldn't have changed, but his thinking, feelings, speech, actions, and rationales were the very likeness of Jesus Christ. Paul was allowing Christ to live His life through him. This, my beloved friends, is not limited to men like the Apostle Paul, but is the very reachable goal for every born-again believer in the Church Age.

> **Galatians 4:19** My little children, of whom I travail in birth again **until Christ be formed in you**, (KJV)

**until Christ be formed in you.** This is a painful verse for those who understand its ramifications. In Paul's mind's-eye, by referring to his target audience as "my little children," he is looking at the Galatian Christians as babes-in-Christ. He realizes that the goal of their Christian lives is to become exactly like Jesus Christ in His humanity. This goal is expressed in the words "until Christ be formed in you." Paul realizes that the road from babyhood to maturity is fraught with circumstances of life, namely, crossroads, forks-in-the-road, and roadblocks, all of which stand as deterrents to reaching Christian maturity. Will they ever reach their goal? The word "until" is a time word and acknowledges that spiritual growth from babyhood to maturity is a process and not something to be reached by a momentary experience, no matter how supernatural the experience may be perceived to be. Will they ever reach their goal? Maybe they will, and maybe they won't, and that's the pain that we read in Paul's use of the word "travail." Paul is saying that the anguish associated with watching a brand new believer move from babyhood to Christian maturity is like experiencing the pain felt by an expectant mother suffering the labor pains of childbirth. The "travail" of which Paul speaks is not the exclusive property of Paul, pastors, preachers, deacons, or other religious servants. This travail belongs to any born-again Christian who has grown sufficiently to know what it takes to get to whatever level of spiritual growth he or she has reached. Then, looking backward from their own level of spiritual growth and seeing others who have not yet advanced to their level, they begin to suffer in "travail," knowing what it will take to reach that higher level. The ultimate goal is "Christ formed in you," fraught with travail in the observer and suffering in the one who is growing.

> **2 Corinthians 3:18** But we all, with open face beholding as in a glass the glory of the Lord, are **changed into the same image** from glory to glory, *even* as by the Spirit of the Lord. (KJV)

**But we all, with open face.** "We" refers to all born-again Church Age believers. "With open face beholding as in a glass" pictures a born-again Church Age believer looking into a mirror and seeing himself for who he really is because he has removed his mask of hypocrisy. The "glass" is a "looking glass," that is, a mirror that reflects an image. In this case, however, the mirror is the mirror of God's Word, the Bible, which reflects the image of Jesus Christ on every page. As the believer looks anywhere in the Bible, and the Holy Spirit illuminates to the believer's mind the image of Christ found on that page, and the next, and the next, and the next, that believer *can be* changed into the image that he sees. This change is said to be from "glory to glory." Every image of Jesus Christ reflects the glory of God the Father, and since spiritual growth is a process from "glory to glory," the indication once again is that spiritual maturity is not reached by a one-shot supernatural experience. The phrase "by the Spirit of the Lord" is a reference to the Holy Spirit. However, here, apo (apo) + the genitive of pneuma (pneuma), is translated "by the Spirit," incorrectly reflecting a genitive of agency, implying that the Holy Spirit is the One who is directly *producing* the outer change observable to the world. The phrase "from glory to glory" represents both epignwsij (epignosis) knowledge being transferred into the new-man's spiritual clothes closet, and from there, replacing old-man clothing on the launching pad of one's heart. To say it another way, this believer is doing the right thing in the right way. He is applying the Word of God to his circumstances of life from the source of his new-man. This is not just a change in thinking, but a change in the way the believer applies because his thinking has changed and because he has determined to live that way. The Holy Spirit manifests Himself in two ways during this process. First, He illuminates the believer's mind to the truth. Second, because this believer is yielded to the Holy Spirit at the fourth step in "Operation KRRY," the believer passively absorbs the Holy Spirit, and the Holy Spirit passively infuses the believer. This results in an organic connection (oneness) of believer and Spirit. From this condition of oneness with the Spirit, the believer then produces the specific thought, feeling, spoken word, overt action, or rationale required for the circumstance of life. apo (apo) + the genitive of pneuma (pneuma) is a genitive of source, not a genitive of agency. This indicates that it is from the "sphere of the Spirit," which is the result of the believer's function in "Operation KRRY," that the manifestations of Christ-likeness occur on these occasions.

> **Philippians 1:21 For to me to live *is* Christ**, and to die *is* gain. (KJV)

**For me to live is Christ.** The goal of the Christian life is expressed again by Paul. For him to live IS Christ. Paul wanted every thought, feeling, spoken word, overt activity, or rationale to be consistent with exactly what Jesus would have done in any given circumstance.

These five verses make it very clear that the goal of the Christian way of life is to become exactly like Christ in His humanity, a very reachable goal.

# Chapter 6

# Christian Maturity Defined and Described

## Introductory Statement

The words definition and description are not necessarily synonymous; therefore, Christian maturity will be defined and described. While much may be found written elsewhere about Christian maturity, it's generally described, but rarely defined. Although the major portion of this chapter is given to description, the definition will be viewed as more important than its description. The description will simply amplify and reinforce the definition.

This chapter purposely contains redundancy and lengthy statements. They are deemed necessary to minimize ambiguity; however, minimization of ambiguity may not result in acceptance of the definition or every part of the descriptive narrative. What will be written is believed to be consistent with biblical truth. The author will rest in his belief that the Holy Spirit is able to confirm both definition and description to his readers' hearts.

Before continuing this chapter, please go to the "Glossary" and read the definitions for the following words: heart, relational strategies, world view, dominance, and non-dominance.

## Christian Maturity Defined

Christian maturity is the spiritual condition of *being* exactly like Jesus Christ in His humanity under any and all conditions and circumstances of life.

## An Incorrect Definition

Christian maturity is the spiritual condition of *becoming* exactly like Jesus Christ in His humanity under any and all conditions and circumstances of life.

## The Difference: Being vs. Becoming

Christian maturity is a goal having been reached, as in *being* like Christ in His humanity under *all* conditions and in *every* circumstance of life. *Becoming* like Christ implies a process under way. Obviously, if the process is under way, the goal has not been reached.

## A Word of Caution: Being vs. Becoming

As a Christian grows toward Christian maturity, every behavioral act accomplished from the source of the new-man is an act of being like Christ in His humanity; however, being like Christ in a single act should not be interpreted as an act being performed by a mature Christian. Single acts are merely a part of the process of becoming like Christ in His humanity as the believer grows from babyhood to adolescence into maturity.

## Definition Restated

Christian maturity is the spiritual condition of *being* exactly like Christ in His humanity under any and all conditions and circumstances of life.

## The Concept of Christian Maturity Expanded in Description

Consider the stages of Christian development toward spiritual maturity as analogous to human development:

brephos (βρεφος)-newborn
nepios (νεπιos)-not yet speaking
pais (παις)-toddler

teknon (τεκνον)-under authority
huios (υιος)-adult son

The mature Christian (huios status) still has old-man relational strategies and old-man world views residing in his heart; however, in huios status, the old-man relational strategies and old-man world views are no longer dominant.

The mature Christian's new-man relational strategies and world views are comprised of the absolute truths in the inspired, inerrant, infallible Word of God.

Christian maturity (huios status) is just as reachable in the spiritual realm as adulthood is in the physical realm.

God the Father does not intend for Christian maturity to be a goal to be shot-at, but unreachable. What kind of a God do we serve who would require us to reach a goal for which He has not already provided the means to reach it? What kind of a Christian are we who would say to God, "I am aware of the provision that you have made for me to become like Christ in His humanity, but I will never be able to use it in such a manner as to become what you want me to be." God forbid!

## Capacity vs. Experience

Capacity for maturity and experiential maturity are not the same. Capacity for maturity is determined by the amount of truth internalized only as far as the new-man's clothes closet. Experiential maturity is determined by the amount of truth on the launching pad of one's soul. This distinction is very helpful in explaining why and how so many Christians have been students of God's Word for years and years, yet give little evidence of Christ-likeness in their moment-by-moment walk. They have built great capacity, but for whatever reason have never moved truth from their new-man's clothes closet to the launching pad. The truths that they hold are in the position of non-dominance rather than the position of dominance.

Capacity for maturity precedes experience. You cannot be like the humanity of Christ in any situation if you do not know how He would respond to a situation.

As a brephos, nepios, pais, or teknon level Christian, you might know how the humanity of Christ would respond in a particular situation, and in fact you might even respond in that manner; however, this would not be a manifestation of the huios in maturity. Christian maturity demands and reflects both knowledge and continual consistent experience (application). The Christian can have capacity without experience, but cannot have experience without capacity.

Christian maturity as a reachable goal in life is preceded by capacity for maturity. Capacity is developed through a knowledge of the Word of God that enables the Christian to be exactly like Christ in His humanity under all conditions and in every circumstance of life. Christian maturity is the status of manifesting agape love toward every member of the human race under all conditions. It also trusts God in every circumstance of life. The greatest manifestations of Christian maturity are agape love toward every member of the human race under all conditions and trusting God in every circumstance of life. Christian maturity does not demand full knowledge of the cause or effect of any condition or circumstance of life, but it does demand the application of agape love or a trust in God.

When new-man relational strategies and new-man world views become dominant, this does not imply that old-man strategies and old-man world views no longer exist in the mature believer's heart. They simply reside subconsciously in the Christian's memory center in a non-dominant role.

The continued existence of old-man relational strategies and old-man world views at a subconscious level in the mature Christian's heart should never be thought to imply that since they continue to exist that one day they will necessarily emerge again as an application in even one circumstance of life. The very reason that the old-man strategies and old-man world views reside in a non-dominant role is because the new-man strategies and new-man world views are being applied habitually. The key word is habitually. This is the same manner that old-man strategies and old-man world views were applied before the new-man strategies and world-views were "put-on." When a new-man strategy and new-man world view become habitually applied, it requires a conscious decision, tantamount to malice aforethought, to take off the new-man strategy or new-man world view to once again put-on an old-man strategy or old-man world view. Theoretically, this could happen, but it's highly unlikely. Why? Because Christian maturity, as a spiritual level already attained, by its very nature has such an inherently high motivational level to love God the Father, to knowingly honor Him, to knowingly have a part in resolving the angelic conflict, to knowingly receive blessing-in-time, and to knowingly receive reward at the bema seat, that when a conscious decision has to be made to set aside the new in favor of the old, that decision would be viewed by the mature Christian as so repugnant that it would be immediately rejected. This is what happens in Christian maturity, but not necessarily before reaching that level. This is what Christian maturity is, and this is what mature Christians do! They reject as repugnant old-man strategies and old-man world views.

Christian maturity is defined as the spiritual condition attained that has resulted in being exactly like Christ in His humanity under any and all conditions and circumstances of life.

# Chapter 7

# The Christian Walk: Formulaic or Logical Progression?

The Christian walk is not formulaic, and with that statement I wholeheartedly agree. The Christian walk is not formulaic, and wasn't intended by God the Father to be so. However, when the statement is made that the Christian walk is not formulaic, it is generally stated derogatorily. The intent is to castigate those who view the Christian walk to be the result of logical progression. The word walk refers to application. Logical progression refers to steps that precede the walk that are required to produce the walk in such a manner that the walk is acceptable to God the Father. Those who castigate are guilty of erroneously equating the decreed logically progressive steps as though they were a legalistic formula.

To fail to correctly differentiate logically progressive steps from formula and then imply that logical progression is tantamount to legalism is to undermine the very nature of God the Father's plan for the Christian's moment-by-moment walk. Again, it treats logical progression as though it were a legalistic old-man strategy.

To define logical progression negatively as being formulaic is to misrepresent the Father's plan, and those who do so are forced to substitute their own plan for how the moment-by-moment Christian walk is to be accomplished. The substitute is often some form of compassionate response toward the hurting people of this world, but offered from the source of the old-man because "Operation KRRY" is by-passed. They offer a "what" without the "how."

The old-man easily views logical progression as formulaic because it's within the scope of old-man nature to think that way. What the old-man doesn't understand is that when the babe-in-Christ first learns "Operation KRRY" as the process by which he is to move from old-man function to new-man function, the babe must break old-man habits. To do so, he must become alert to both the circumstances of life that trigger old-man function and the process designed by God the Father to do so. For example, as soon as the Christian begins to recognize the circumstance that triggers an old-man function, he must Know, he must Reckon, he must Reckon, and he must Yield-and in that order. This process is not a legalistic formula. It's the logical progression of cognitive learning skills decreed by God the Father in eternity past. However, when the old-man listens to the babe verbalizing the cognitive learning process, "First, I must *know* that my old-man was crucified with Christ; second, I must *reckon* myself dead to sin; third, I must *reckon* my new-man alive to God; and fourth, I must *yield* to God the Holy Spirit," the old-man says, "Gotcha! See there? I told you that what you call logical progression is legalistic formula. You said, 'First, second, third, fourth, and if that isn't formulaic, I don't know what is.'"

Here's the problem. The old-man doesn't understand the divinely decreed cognitive learning pattern by which a babe-in-Christ breaks an old-man habit and develops a new-man habit. If he did understand, he'd realize that each step enumerated by the babe-in-Christ is not some scatter-brained legalistic formula, but a recollection of the correct cognitive learning process by which a habit is formed.

When the Christian becomes alert to the circumstances of life that trigger old-man functions, he can begin to use the logically progressive steps of "Operation KRRY" to break old-man habits and replace them with a new-man habits. This is the only means by which God-honoring victory is achieved.

# Section 3

# How the Christian Way of Life Works

# Chapter 8

# "Operation KRRY" Is the Answer

## Two "If's" and Three Questions

If the "big picture" of life is the resolution of the spiritual battle referred to as the angelic conflict, and if the goal of every human being in the Church Age is to become exactly like Christ in His humanity, the latter "if" raises three big questions. First, is becoming like Christ in His humanity even possible? Second, if it is, how is it accomplished? Third, did I say human race or did I mean to say Christian? Let me deal with the last question first.

## Third Question First

Did I say human race or did I mean to say Christian? Yes, I said and meant human race. The human race was created by Jesus Christ according to God the Father's plan for the purpose of resolving the angelic conflict. At the moment of physical birth, every human being is drafted into the conflict. They don't enlist. Enlistment is a choice. There is no choice when drafted. By divine decree every human being is drafted into the conflict. The question regards the side on which the human being is going to serve-God's or Satan's? The Dispensation of the Church Age does not free the human race from its obligation to resolve the conflict. The Church Age portion of human history merely points the human race to Christianity as the holder of the only means by which the conflict can be resolved during this dispensation. Christianity is unique is this manner. Whatever the world view happens to be about numerous world religions, Christianity is the sole possessor of the guidelines for resolving the angelic conflict during this dispensation. This is why it's so vitally important for mankind, not just Christians, to understand the angelic conflict. Until the resolution of this conflict is clearly understood as the reason for the existence of the human race, Christianity is perceived by the world as just one religion among many, any one believed to be just as good as the other–so just take your choice. God forbid!

Christianity is not a religion. It is a personal relationship with God the Father through God the Son, Jesus Christ. Until members of the human race become born-again Christians, no matter how religious, how nice, how kind, how wonderful they might be, they remain condemned to the lake of fire. Their method of worshipping their "god" resolves no part of the angelic conflict and is their ticket to an eternal separation from the Eternal God whose plan they have rejected.

# First Question

Is becoming like Christ in His humanity even possible? The answer is not just, yes, but emphatically, yes! How is it accomplished? The remainder of this chapter is designed to answer that question.

The following list provides both the logical and chronological order of God the Father's decreed design for every member of the human race to become exactly like Jesus Christ in His humanity: spiritual salvation, clean before the Lord, the function of "Operation KRRY," and doing the truth.

## Step One

Spiritual salvation as the first step occurs the moment a member of the human race places his personal faith-alone in Christ-alone. Salvation is not achieved by some form of works; for example, no one has every been saved by water baptism, walking an aisle, praying the sinner's prayer, speaking in tongues, joining the church, confessing sins, praying through, or by any other form of human effort. For emphasis, spiritual salvation is not achieved by a system of human works. Salvation comes by faith-alone in Christ-alone. It is grievously sad to listen to some Christians claim that they agree that salvation is by grace through faith, and then claim that water baptism is required for salvation. Their old-man thinking goes like this. God's grace provision for spiritual salvation includes water baptism, and they are placing their faith in that grace provision. Therefore, they erroneously conclude that they are saved by grace through faith. Faith is not their problem. It's the object of their faith that has distorted God's grace provision. Baptismal regeneration, whether by sprinkling, pouring, or immersing is human work all-the-way. It adds human effort to the finished work of Jesus Christ on Calvary's cross. It distorts God's grace provision and is a certain ticket to the lake of fire for all who have never placed their faith in anything other than this distorted means of spiritual salvation.

Spiritual salvation is the result of trusting that Jesus Christ was crucified, died spiritually, died physically, was buried, and was resurrected three days later. His resurrection from among the dead makes Him unique among all who have founded a religion. All other founders remain in the grave awaiting their resurrection and one-on-one meeting with Jesus Christ at the great white throne judgment. This occurs at the end of human history at which time they will be banished to the eternal lake of fire. Question: Have you been born-again? If not, why not? Spiritual salvation is the first step in the process of your becoming like Jesus Christ in His humanity. Salvation is received simply by trusting in the Lord Jesus Christ and eternal salvation will be yours. Some have responded, "But that's too easy." My response: "Ask Jesus how easy it was."

## Step Two

Being clean before the Lord is the second step to becoming like Christ in His humanity. The moment you are saved, God the Father *experientially* forgives every sin you have ever committed from the time you were born physically until the moment of your salvation. That portion of your life is now clean before the Lord, and there is no reason for any born-again Christian to ever make pre-salvation sins an issue as though God has not adequately dealt with them as a result of their faith-alone in Christ-alone. Now, after salvation, it's a matter of cleaning up your post-salvation sin account. Christ's substitutionary death on the cross not only paid for your pre-salvation sins, it also paid for your post-salvation sins. This is why every member of the human race stands *judicially* forgiven, but is in need of *experiential* forgiveness. Your *judicial* forgiveness is part of God's grace provision for the human race, but you must accept it. The entire human race stands *judicially* forgiven whether anyone chooses to accept that forgiveness or not. God does not impose Himself on anyone against personal will. God makes the provision, but human beings must choose to accept.

Post-salvation sins are forgiven through the application of 1 John 1:9 to the personal Christian life. The key word in this verse is "confess." It means to name, cite, identify. If you commit a post-salvation sin, that sin is *experientially* cleansed and forgiven the moment you name it to God the Father. "Father, I lied." It stands forgiven. "Father, I became angry." It stands forgiven. No matter what the sin, no matter how heinous the sin, when you name it, you stand immediately *experientially* cleansed and forgiven of that sin. For the Christian to be *experientially* clean before the Lord after salvation, it's imperative to confess known sins. You cannot confess unknown sins or sins forgotten. Forgotten sins are treated by God as unknown to you. When you confess all known sins committed since your previous time of confession, God *experientially* cleanses and forgives not only your known sins but your unknown sins also. Now, at that moment, you are experientially clean before the Lord.

## Step Three

The third step is "Operation KRRY," an acrostic representing a four step process: know, reckon, reckon, and yield. The concept is found in the language of Romans 6:6, 11, and 13 in the King James Version. Let's consider "Operation KRRY."

> Romans 6:6 *Knowing* this, that our old man is crucified with him, that the body of sin might be destroyed, that henceforth we should not serve sin. (KJV)

> Romans 6:11 Likewise *reckon* ye also yourselves to be dead indeed unto sin, but [*reckon* ye also yourselves to be] alive unto God through Jesus Christ our Lord. (KJV)

> Romans 6:13 Neither yield ye your members as instruments of unrighteousness unto sin: but *yield* yourselves unto God, as those that are alive from the dead, and your members as instruments of righteousness unto God. (KJV)

First, Paul tells us in Romans 6:6 that Christians should *know* something. This is the "K" part of "Operation KRRY."

> **Romans 6:6 *Knowing* this** [namely, that our old man WAS crucified with Christ; this is referred to as co-crucifixion]**, that our** [Church Age believer's] **old man** [the personification of the soul when yielded to the body's sinful nature] **is** [literally, was] **crucified** [put to death] **with** [in association with; on the same cross with; at the same time in history as] **him** [Jesus Christ]**, that the body** [the physical body] **of** [possessing] **sin** [a sinful nature] **might be destroyed** [rendered inoperative]**, that** [introduces the purpose for which the old man was

crucified with Christ] **henceforth** [from that time forward] **we** [Church Age believers] **should not** [should no longer be required to] **serve** [be slaves to] **sin** [the sinful nature]. (KJV)

Man is born a slave to his sinful nature; however, this verse tells us that God the Father has decreed a plan whereby no human being is required to continue in that slavery. In fact, using God's plan, you never have to sin again. If man is to break away from that slavery, there are some things he must understand. What is the old-man? What is co-crucifixion? What is the meaning of "might be destroyed?"

**What Is the "Old-Man?"**

Old-man is a term first used by the Apostle Paul to describe the source of all human function prior to the moment of spiritual salvation. Assume for a moment that you talking about some non-Christian, and you observe some form of his thought, feeling, speech, overt action, or rationalization, and you ask yourself the question, "Where did that come from?" The answer is that it came from his old-man. What, then, is the old-man?

There are two words used in conjunction with the term "old-man" that will answer this question. The two words are *abstract* and *personify*. The word abstract means something that actually exists, but is imperceptible to sight, hearing, feeling, smelling, or taste. The word personify means an abstraction represented as having personality, that is, as though the abstraction were able to think, feel, speak, act, or reason. Personification treats an abstraction as though it were a real person. Now, let's apply these two words to the "old-man."

The old-man is an abstraction that is personified. This means that he exists, but you can't see, hear, feel, smell, or taste him. He exists as a personification. This means that this abstract old-man is treated as though he were a real person capable of thought, feeling, speech, overt action, and rationalization.

When the human soul is operating under the influence of the human body's sinful nature, and the human body parts are manifesting thought, feeling, speech, overt action, or rationalizations, it is said that it's the old-man that is producing these things. It's actually you who are doing these things. It's you who are thinking, you who are feeling, you who are speaking, you who are doing, you who are rationalizing; but these actions are explained as old-man functions because you have chosen to yield your soul to your body's sinful nature.

**Default Function-No Other Options.** From birth to salvation, the human soul functions by *default* under the influence of the human body's sinful nature because it has no other immediate option. This means that old-man function is the *default* mode of every human being until saved.

**What Is Co-Crucifixion?** This term means that two persons are crucified simultaneously. The two persons are Jesus Christ and the personified "old-man" of every born-again Christian. Let that sink in. This is God the Father's decreed plan, and until this is clearly understood, there is absolutely no basis for total victory over personal sins in a Christian's life. The Christian must come to grips with the fact that his old-man has been crucified WITH Christ. If you know that your old-man is the immediate source of every personal sin that you commit, and God says your old-man is dead, the question is this. How much sin can a dead man commit? The answer is none! If this is so, another legitimate question might be, "Then why do I continue to commit personal sins if my old-man has been crucified with Christ?" The answer to that question is forthcoming. Just remember this, at this point it's only God the Father who says your old-man WAS crucified with Christ. You haven't yet spoken on this matter.

**What is "the body of sin?"** The phrase "body of sin" can be translated "sinful body" emphasizing the intrinsically sinful nature of the human body. Intrinsic means essential to the nature of a thing. Every human being needs to come to grips with this. Look in the mirror. The very nature of the body at which you are looking is sinful by nature. This is not because you've done anything wrong. It's because you were born into the human race, and you had nothing to do with that. Your very nature is fallen because of the fall of Adam and Eve in the Garden of Eden. Every living thing is born after its own kind. Using this principle, sinful man begets sinful children; so, here we are-sinful human beings. Caution: The human body does not have an old-sin-nature in the sense that the old-sin-nature is one thing and the human body is another, totaling two different things. No, not two things, but one. The human body is intrinsically sinful. It's the very nature of the human body to be sinful, trending away from God, not toward Him. When you think of the human body you must think of more than what you can see. It includes every internal organ, every fiber of its being, including the brain. The sinful human body influences the human soul. The body craves, wants, desires and volition yields. Hence, until a man becomes born-again during the Church Age, the soul's self-consciousness is egocentric; the soul's mentality is filled with old-man thinking; the volition yields to the sinful nature; the soul's emotions are negative; and the soul's conscience is filled with false norms and standards. You are totally depraved. You have nothing to offer God the Father that He can accept.

**What Is the Meaning of "Might Be Destroyed?"** Here's how that phrase is rendered in popular versions of the Bible.

> might be destroyed (KJV)
> might be done away with (NKJV)
> might be done away with (NASB)
> might be done away with (NIV)
> might lose its power (NLT)
> a decisive end to that sin-miserable life (The Message)
> might be made ineffective and inactive (Amplified Bible)

Might be destroyed? No, not destroyed. This leads to the erroneous theological position of one naturism that rejects the old-man new-man concept. Might be destroyed? No. This phrase translates the aorist, passive, subjunctive of the word καταργεω (katargeo). Yes, this word has several different meanings: to make ineffective, powerless, idle; abolish, wipe out, set aside; to be released from an association with someone or something, have nothing to do with. Interpreters will choose a definition consistent with their paradigm. I will do the same. If God intended for the sinful nature to be destroyed, Satan would have a valid argument against the justice (fairness) of God. He might say, "You created man to resolve this conflict. Now, You've removed his sinful nature, and look at him. He's a robot. He couldn't do anything wrong if he wanted to, and I'm headed to the lake of fire because he's the lower creature and doing everything right. And You're telling people that You're just (fair). You've gotta' be kiddin' me." Satan would be right; however, the old-man has not been destroyed. Well, if it hasn't been destroyed, then what really happened to it?

I will interpret this aorist, passive, subjunctive of καταργεω (katargeo) as "might be rendered inoperative." God the Father has decreed that the sinful nature MIGHT be rendered inoperative. The word MIGHT is important. It indicates that the sinful nature has not yet been rendered *experientially* inoperative-positionally inoperative, yes; experientially inoperative, no. God the Father rendered it inoperative positionally by decreeing it co-crucified with Christ. Now, it's the Christian's turn. Maybe he will, and maybe he won't. Therein, lays the MIGHT of it. The choice belongs to the born-again Christian. Complete the four step process of

"Operation KRRY" and *experiential* victory becomes a reality and places MIGHT in the ash heap where it belongs.

Second, Paul speaks of two forms of *reckoning* in Romans 6:11: *reckon* dead and *reckon* alive. These are the two "R's" of "Operation KRRY."

> **Romans 6:11 Likewise** [in the same manner as God the Father thinks] ***reckon*** [consider] **ye** [Church Age believers] **also yourselves** [Church Age believers] **to be dead** [incapable of producing personal sins; this is the experiential side of Romans 6:6; this is the believer treating his old-man as dead because God says it is dead] **indeed unto sin** [the sinful nature]**, but** [*reckon* ye also yourselves to be] **alive** [spiritually] **unto God** [the Father] **through Jesus Christ our** [Church Age believers] **Lord. (KJV)**

The word *reckon* means to consider, to think the same way God thinks; and in this verse God is thinking two different ways. If you think the same way God thinks, you will *reckon* yourself dead to the sinful nature followed by *reckoning* yourself alive unto God. The second *reckon* is elliptical, meaning it isn't stated directly, but is understood as though it had been stated. If you as a Christian fail to acknowledge the elliptical *reckon* and apply only the first, you will be guilty of doing what Miles Stanford referred to as half-reckoning in his book, *The Reckoning That Counts,* p. 36. You will *reckon* yourself dead to sin, but fail to *reckon* yourself alive unto God. This is half-reckoning which is tantamount to old-man thinking because it doesn't match the truth; and no matter how much you apply while half-reckoning, what you apply is no more than old-man function that is worthless to both you and God in the resolution of the spiritual battle known as the angelic conflict. What makes anyone believe that if we don't do what God wants His way that somehow or another He's going to overlook our ignorance or unwillingness to fully cooperate with Him? Remember, the angelic conflict is the backdrop against which all of human life is to be lived and measured, and God isn't interested in you doing His thing your way if your way does not match His way. "But you are a God of love," you might say, to which He will respond, "Yes, but I am also a righteous and just God, and when you fail to abide by my plan, your negative decision will require my righteousness to reject your negativity and my justice will be required to discipline you–and I'll be loving you all-the-while."

*Twice-reckoning* is simply agreeing with God about your old-man and your new-man. You agree that your old-man who is influenced by your sinful nature is your problem and that your new-man influenced by the Holy Spirit is your solution.

# Enter the Concept of Dominance

Again, Miles Stanford speaks of the reckoning that counts. In fact, it's the title of one of his books. Borrowing that phrase, the reckoning that counts implies three things: understanding, believing, and dominance. Understanding simply means to know what someone has conveyed. Understanding is a must, but it is worthless when standing alone. Believing implies trusting what is understood. Believing is an absolute must, but it is worthless when joined to understanding without being joined to dominance. Dominance refers to a position. It refers to the launching pad of the soul, the location from which all application is made to the circumstances of your life. For any given circumstance, either an old-man strategy or a new-man strategy is in the position of dominance; and whichever strategy is dominant is what you will apply at the appropriate moment. The particular strategy that you determine to apply is on the launching pad by your choice. It didn't just slip-up on you without your choosing to place it there at sometime in your life.

Dominant twice-reckoning means that you have chosen to remove from the launching pad the old-man strategy that previously dominated your thought, and you have replaced it with its new-man clothing counterpart. You have placed "twice-reckoning" on the launching pad of your soul's mentality. You might ask yourself a question. "What process have I previously used to deal with the circumstances of my life?" If it is anything other than twice-reckoning, it's time for a change. Make reckoning your old-man dead to its sinful influence and reckoning your new-man alive unto God the habit of your spiritual practice. In this, you will have completed the process of understanding, believing, and making twice-reckoning dominant in your life. Whatever is dominant in your spiritual life is what you will apply, and until "twice-reckoning" is in the dominant position, whatever strategy you apply will be applied from the source of your old-man, and this is spiritual disaster.

Third, Paul tells us in Romans 6:13 that Christians should *yield* themselves unto God, and their members (body parts) as instruments of righteousness unto God. This is the "Y" part of "Operation KRRY."

**Romans 6:13 Neither** [do not] **yield** [present] **ye** [Church Age believers] **your** [Church Age believer's] **members** [body parts: hands, feet, eyes, ears, tongue, etc.] **as instruments** [tools] **of unrighteousness** [that which is contrary to the goodness of God] **unto sin** [the sinful nature]**: but** *yield* [present] **yourselves** [Church Age believers] **unto God** [the Holy Spirit]**, as those** [Church Age believers] **that** [who] **are** [spiritually] **alive from the** [spiritually] **dead, and** [present] **your** [Church Age believer's] **members** [body parts: hands, feet, eyes, ears, tongue, etc.] **as instruments** [tools] **of** [associated with] **righteousness** [the absolute goodness of God] **unto God** [God the Holy Spirit]**. (KJV)**

Note that the born-again Christian can *yield* in one of two directions. One option is to *yield* to sin, that is, to his sinful nature, or the other option is to *yield* to God. To *yield* to sin is described as *yielding* your body parts as tools of unrighteousness. This means presenting your body parts to the sinful nature so that they can be used as tools to produce personal sins or human good. To *yield* to God is described as yielding your body parts to God as tools of righteousness. This means presenting your body parts to God so that they can be used as tools to produce divinely righteous functions.

Even though the Christian *knows* that God says his old-man is dead, and even though the Christian *reckons* his old-man dead, and even though the Christian *reckons* his new-man alive unto God, there can be no victory over the sinful nature unless the Christian makes a decision to *yield* himself and his body parts to God the Holy Spirit. The Christian must Know, Reckon, Reckon, and YIELD.

Conclusion: Knowing, reckoning, reckoning, and yielding is the process of "Operation KRRY" and "Operation KRRY" is the only divine tool given to the Christian whereby God the Father is honored when personal victory is experientially gained over the Christian's sinful nature.

The next major topic deals with *suffering* associated with twice-reckoning and yielding. Here, we'll learn that all suffering does not mean that you are doing something wrong.

# Twice-Reckoning and Yielding Produce Suffering

It must be understood that the believer will suffer while twice-reckoning and yielding. Listen and comprehend that statement. The believer WILL suffer while twice-reckoning and yielding. Suffering is experienced because something is being done right, not because something is being done wrong. When the old-man is being reckoned dead, he doesn't accept his death easily. He struggles to stay alive, and it is this struggle that causes the believer to suffer. What is this suffering? It's an emotion interpreted by the human mind and experienced as mental anguish associated with turning away from an old-man function and turning to a new-man function.

If the old-man would just roll over and die without incident, the spiritual battle would be won without suffering, but it doesn't happen that way. The suffering associated with twice-reckoning and yielding is a clear indication that God plans for the old-man to be reckoned dead without spiritual anesthesia. Therefore, twice-reckoning and yielding spontaneously produce suffering associated with old-man death. He goes down swinging. Suffering is associated with doing the right-thing in the right-way.

## Confession vs. "Operation KRRY"

What is the difference between confession and "Operation KRRY?" Remember that both confession and "Operation KRRY" have a relationship to personal sin. Confession is the remedy for personal sin *after* sin has been committed. "Operation KRRY" is the remedy for personal sin *before* the sin has been committed. Confession results in cleansing and forgiveness of unrighteousness (whatever sin has been confessed). "Operation KRRY" restores the believer to fellowship with God and then maintains the progress of fellowship as long as the concept of "Operation KRRY" is retained in the place of dominance. It should be clear that God desires the Church Age believer to deal with personal sin *before* the fact, rather than *after* the fact.

Perhaps this illustration will help. Suppose you have a horse that constantly escapes from its barn, and every time it escapes it injures itself. Confession is like treating the injury without returning the horse to the barn. "Operation KRRY" returns the healed horse to the barn and provides a solution whereby the horse need never escape again.

Conclusion: God the Father is far more interested in the horse never escaping the barn than He is in having to heal an injured horse before returning it to the barn.

# Mortify Your Members and "Operation KRRY"

The following two verses are quoted from three different versions of the Bible: the King James Version, the New American Standard Version, and the New International Version. Key words have been underlined. These words represent God's plan for dealing with personal sin in the life of the Church Age believer. They are associated with "Operation KRRY."

## Colossians 3:5

Colossians 3:5 <u>Mortify</u> therefore your members which are upon the earth; fornication, uncleanness, inordinate affection, evil concupiscence, and covetousness, which is idolatry: (KJV)

Colossians 3:5 Therefore <u>consider</u> the members of your earthly body <u>as dead</u> to immorality, impurity, passion, evil desire, and greed, which amounts to idolatry. (NAS)

Colossians 3:5 <u>Put to death,</u> therefore, whatever belongs to your earthly nature: sexual immorality, impurity, lust, evil desires and greed, which is idolatry. (NIV)

Under the inspiration of the Holy Spirit, the Apostle Paul has listed certain personal sins. Compare the three versions:

| KJV | NAS | NIV |
|---|---|---|
| fornication | immorality | sexual immorality |
| uncleanness | impurity | impurity |
| inordinate affection | passion | lust |
| evil concupiscence | evil desire | evil desire |
| covetousness | greed | greed |

Paul then declares God's plan for dealing with them.

| KJV | NAS | NIV |
|---|---|---|
| mortify | consider as dead | put to death |

*Wuest's Word Studies*, Volume 1, "Colossians," p. 219, addresses this verse:

> "God in salvation has broken the power of the evil nature over the believer's physical body. Now, the believer is charged with the responsibility of maintaining in his experience that state of liberation, and, as the behests of the evil nature come before him, he is to put them to death, that is refuse to obey them."

Please note that Wuest wants to put to death the *behests* of the evil nature. The word behests refers to personal sins that one might be tempted to commit. Wuest has missed the point. We are not to put personal sins to death. We are to reckon the old-man dead to sin. Personal sins are manifestations of yieldedness to the sinful nature. It's the sinful nature that is the problem, not personal sins. Here's an analogy. If you have a spider web in the corner of a ceiling, and you want to permanently rid yourself of the spider web, you don't sweep away the spider web. It'll be back tomorrow, the next day, and the next day if you just keep sweeping. You kill the spider. By analogy, the spider is the sinful nature, and the spider web represents personal sins. Although God the Father has given us a plan to deal with personal sins *after* the fact, He has also given us a plan to deal with personal sins *before* the fact. His plan is to deal with personal sins at the level of spider-source, i.e., the sinful nature reckoned dead because he has pronounced it judicially dead.

My observation has been that multitudes of Christians are trying to get victory over personal sins with an old-man strategy, namely, working on *putting to death* every personal sin that comes before them. As victorious and hopeful as this may appear, working at putting personal sin to death doesn't work because that's an old-man solution the result of believing that that's how victory is gained. You don't have to put anything to death by means of human effort; and even if you did gain momentary victory, it wouldn't last. That's tantamount to a success-failure story-momentary success, but failure in that it was victory accomplished the wrong way. It was human effort victory vs. failure to trust in God's provision. We are to reckon the old-man dead, reckon the new-man alive, yield to the Spirit, and do the truth! Bingo!! Victory God's way in the angelic conflict.

## Romans 8:13

> Romans 8:13 For if ye live after the flesh, ye shall die: but if ye through the Spirit do *mortify* the deeds of the body, ye shall live. (KJV)

> Romans 8:13 for if you are living according to the flesh, you must die; but if by the Spirit you are putting to death the deeds of the body, you will live. (NAS)

> Romans 8:13 For if you live according to the sinful nature, you will die; but if by the Spirit you put to death the misdeeds of the body, you will live, (NIV)

Both Colossians 3:5 and Romans 8:13 in the King James Version use the word *mortify* to describe what the believer is to do to deal with the sinful nature of his life. The New American Standard says, "consider as dead" and "putting to death." The New International Version says, "put to death." All of these terms imply the process of "Operation KRRY."

## Concluding Thought

The terminology of Colossians 3:5 and Romans 8:13 is disastrous to Christian spirituality if the following thought is not understood, believed, and placed in the position of dominance. The terms *mortify, consider as dead*, and *putting to death* MUST be understood as terms that tell the Christian WHAT-to-do. They do not tell the Christian HOW-to-do what he is being told to do. *Mortify, consider as dead*, and *put to death* are WHAT you are to do to get victory over your sinful nature. "Operation KRRY" tells you HOW you mortify, how you consider as dead, how you put to death your sinful nature. The WHAT without the HOW produces nothing but misery in this temporal life and generates nothing but wood hay, and stubble works that will burn at the bema seat of Christ. What a shame, simply because Christians fail to understand or reject God's provision of "Operation KRRY."

# Chapter 9

# Do the Truth

In 1969, my family and I lived in Forth Worth, Texas. I was in seminary at the time. My wife and I were privileged to meet a lady who impacted our lives spiritually. One of her sayings went like this: "Do the truth." That statement was indelibly imprinted in my mind, and it frequently comes to mind as I think of the necessity of doing what is right. This is an injunction that every Christian needs to hear and heed.

What does it mean to "do the truth?" The fourth step in "Operation KRRY" is to yield to the Spirit. This yieldedness results in the condition of the believer being "in the Spirit;" however, life doesn't end there. The believer must learn to distinguish two terms that describe a born-again Christian's spiritual condition: spiritual and carnal. Every born-again Christian has eternal life, but the condition of the Christian life is either spiritual or carnal. Paul makes these two distinctions in 1 Corinthians 2:15 and 1 Corinthians 3:1. The spiritual believer functions "in the Spirit" and produces new-man functions. The carnal believer functions "in the flesh" and produces old-man functions.

Great caution needs to be taken here. Both the carnal believer and the spiritual believer can observably do exactly the same thing, but only the effort of the spiritual believer meets the approval of God the Father. Someone might say, "But they're both doing the truth," and that would be absolutely correct; however, the Church Age believer is required to do more than just do-the-truth. He must do-the-truth in the right way. I refer to this as doing the right thing in the right way. The right-thing is doing the divine imperative and not doing the divine prohibition. The right-way is function from the position of "in the Spirit." This is what new-man function is. It's doing the right thing in the right-way

This brings the believer's royal priesthood and royal ambassadorship into the picture. As a royal priest, the believer represents himself before God. As a royal ambassador, the believer represents God before his fellow man. Both priesthood and ambassadorship are new-man functions; and yes, the old-man can imitate new-man function, but an imitation is never the real deal. An imitation is doing the right-thing in the wrong-way, and the wrong-way is from the source of the old-man. While you and I might not be able to tell the difference between the imitation and the genuine, God can, and He's the One who counts the most.

So, if you are told that you need to do-the-truth, you need to be aware of the fact that doing the truth is the step that follows "Operation KRRY." Here it is, pure and simple. You become saved; you assure yourself that you are cleansed from all post-salvation sins; you know that your old-man was crucified with Christ; you reckon your old-man dead to sin; you reckon your new-man alive unto God; you yield to the Holy Spirit, and now, YOU DO THE TRUTH! It's only when the truth is done in this manner that the believer has spiritual impact and that his efforts are blessable in time, rewardable in eternity, and God-honoring.

# Chapter 10

# The Concepts of Internalization and Actualization

## Internalization and Actualization

*Internalization* is a vocabulary term used to describe the process of moving truth from the printed pages of the Bible onto the launching pad of the spiritual heart. *Internalization* as a process is not complete until truth has been placed on the launching pad. *Actualization* is a vocabulary term used to describe two events: 1) launching previously internalized pertinent truth from the launching pad as an application to a life situation; and 2) the manifestation of a Christ-like example seen or heard by anyone in the periphery of the *actualization* (application).

In this chapter, as we follow the process of internalization and actualization, there are two necessary assumptions: 1) during the internalization process, the believer is clean before the Lord through confession of post-salvation sins (1 John 1:9), and is wanting to want God's good pleasure for his life (Philippians 2:13); and 2) during the process of actualization, the believer is functioning from the source of the new-man while in the Spirit as a result of functioning in "Operation KRRY."

The process of internalization demands total openness to the teaching of God's Word accompanied by a desire to know and apply the truth.

**1 Peter 2:2 As newborn babes, desire the sincere milk of the word, that ye may grow thereby: (KJV)**

The word "desire" is a command. This means that Christians are commanded by God the Father to "long for" truth found in the inspired, inerrant, and infallible Word of God. Why? The answer is for spiritual growth, and spiritual growth cannot be accomplished without the internalization and actualization of the Word of God.

Unless there is a total commitment to truth, *internalization* can be interrupted at any time during the process and *actualization* will never occur unless the process of *internalization* is resumed and completed.

What follows will trace the internalization of truth from the printed pages of the Bible to actualization in a life situation. To simplify an understanding of this process, there will be no discussion of the multifarious variations of possibilities. The intent is to demonstrate the process of internalization and actualization in the life of a born-again Christian whose passionate desire and sole focus is to honor God through the internalization and actualization of His Word to the point of reaching the goal of Christ-likeness in Christian maturity.

**Internalization**

To better understand the process of internalization, it will help to list the three major centers (1, 2, 3) and four sub-centers (sub1, sub2, sub3, sub4) in the conscious mind where truth is stored:

(νους).
   1.  reference center.
(καρδια).
   2.  memory center.
       sub1    vocabulary center.
       sub2    category center.
           old-man clothes closet.
           new-man clothes closet.
       sub3    conscience center.
   3.  launching center.
       sub4    growth center.

In this scenario, it is assumed that the believer is clean before the Lord and wanting to want the good pleasure of God for his life before the process of internalization begins.

Truth begins on the printed pages of the Bible as academic information. The Greek word for truth at this point in the internalizing process is λογος (logos).

From the printed pages, truth first enters the section of the conscious mind that the biblical Greek calls the νους. The νους contains a storage center referred to as the reference center. Truth enters the reference center through the ear gate and/or eye gate of those who can see and hear, or tactilely for those who are deaf-blind. The Greek word for truth at this point in the process remains λογος (logos). It is still no more than academic information.

From the reference center, truth moves into the human spirit where the Holy Spirit resides and from which location He initiates His teaching ministry. The Greek word for truth at this point in the process changes to πνευματικος (pneumatikos). This indicates that truth has now become spiritual phenomena because it has been directly affected by the teaching ministry Holy Spirit.

From the human spirit, truth then moves back to the reference center because the human mind is decreed as responsible to make humanly understandable what the Holy Spirit has been teaching the human spirit. The Greek word for truth at this point in the process is γνωσις (gnosis) and refers to truth understood because the human mind has come to understand what the Spirit has been teaching. This is your "ah-ha" moment. Although truth is now understood, understanding and believing are NOT synonymous. Believing what is understood is the next step in the process.

From the reference center, "ah-ha" moment truth believed now moves into the spiritual heart (καρδια) where the remaining two major storage centers are located: the memory center and the launching center.

The memory center is where truth is now referred to as epignwsij (epignosis) meaning full knowledge. επιγνωσις (epignosis) is simply γνωσις (gnosis) truth that has moved from the reference center to the memory center because γνωσις (gnosis) truth has been mixed with faith (believed, trusted).

The moment truth enters the memory center it is distributed to the following sub-centers:

> The vocabulary center where incoming truth is stored as words and phrases to be used in communication.
> The category center containing two clothes closets where definitions and descriptions of the words in the vocabulary center are developed into doctrines: 1) a new-man's clothes closet, and 2) an old-man's clothes closet.
> ➤ Truths that have been confirmed by the Holy Spirit's teaching in the human spirit are stored in the category center's new-man clothes closet as absolute truths.
> ➤ Distorted truths are stored in the old-man's clothes closet as evil principles.

The growth center contains only new-man truth; however, this center contains no truth until new-man truth is moved from the new-man's clothes closet to the launching pad; spiritual growth is determined by the amount of new-man truth on the launching pad.
The conscience center contains a copy of every piece of data received into the memory center; this data forms a believer's norms and standards.

The launching center contains the launching pad from which place all actualization (application) is made to life's situations. The launching pad can contain both old-man beliefs and new-man beliefs.

**Actualization**

Truth is *actualized* (applied) when a circumstance of life calling for an application of pertinent truth from the launching pad is actually applied to the circumstance. Truth cannot be *actualized* from anywhere except the launching pad no matter where it might be located in the process of *internalization* if that location falls short of reaching the launching pad. Since the goal of the Christian life is to reproduce the likeness of Christ in every given life situation, *actualization* includes the example of Christ's life being witnessed by others as that witness is being manifested by the Christian who is making pertinent application of truth to the circumstance of life.

# Section 4

# The Old-man New-man in the Christian Way of Life

# Chapter 11

# Old-man New-man Concepts

The concepts of old-man and new-man are biblically founded. The following passages establish the concepts:

> Romans 6:6 Knowing this, that our **old man** is crucified with him, that the body of sin might be destroyed, that henceforth we should not serve sin. (KJV)

> Ephesians 4:22 That ye put off concerning the former conversation the **old man**, which is corrupt according to the deceitful lusts; (KJV)

> Colossians 3:9 Lie not one to another, seeing that ye have put off the **old man** with his deeds; (KJV)

> Ephesians 4:24 And that ye put on the **new man**, which after God is created in righteousness and true holiness. (KJV)

> Colossians 3:10 And have put on the **new man**, which is renewed in knowledge after the image of him that created him: (KJV)

## Understanding the Old-man and New-man Concepts

Two words help us to understand these two concepts. The words are "abstract" and "personify." The word "abstract" means "to consider apart from concrete existence." This means that you cannot see, hear, feel, smell, or touch the old-man or the new-man, yet, they exist in reality. The word "personify" means "to think of an abstraction as having the qualities of a living being." Using these two definitions, we now know that the old-man and new-man are personifications. They exist as abstractions, but are treated as though they are real persons.

## When Do the Old-Man and New-Man Come into Existence?

The terms old-man and new-man are found only in the Pauline Epistles. This might lead one to conclude that the concepts of old-man and new-man did not exist prior to Paul's disclosure or prior to the importance of Church Age involvement in the resolution of the angelic conflict. These conclusions are understandable, but they might beg-the-question? Is it possible that either the old-man or new-man might have existed prior to Pauline revelation? The answer is yes for the old-man and no for the new-man. Each of the four dispensations and their respective rules for living are associated with the resolution of the angelic conflict. Until the Church Age, the angelic conflict was being resolved by human obedience to the specific rules associated with their respective dispensation. This obedience required no more that human effort. It required no spiritual power. This obedience was obedience while functioning under the influence of the body's sinful nature. It's not until the Church Age that the standard for resolution is human function from a source known as the new-man. To function from the source of the new-man is to not function from the source of the old-man. The concepts are mutually exclusive. Function from both sources simultaneously in a specific circumstance is impossible.

Since the new-man concept is associated with Christ-likeness in the life of the born-again Christian, and nothing like this was ever required in previous dispensations, this implies that the new-man concept is specifically Church Age related. There was no new-man function prior to the Church Age. However, function similar to that of the old-man described by the Apostle Paul certainly existed as far back as fallen man functioning inside the Garden of Eden. If the old-man is the personification of the human soul under the influence of the sinful nature, the question might be asked, "Did anyone living during the two dispensations prior to the Church Age ever function while their soul was under the influence of the sinful nature?" The answer is yes. Hence, if for no reason other than inference, it can be established that the old-man has existed since the fall of man in the Garden of Eden. If so, then why is the old-man never mentioned in the Old Testament? There is no reason to mention him until an alternative is in place. That alternative was made known to the Apostle

Paul as part of progressive revelation. It seems that to argue that the old-man was non-existent during the Age of the Gentiles and the Age of Israel based upon the silence of Scripture would also require the rejection of any inductive conclusion from ever entering the Christian's system of theology. Why? Because the nature of inductive conclusions is that they have no single proof-text?

The old-man has existed since the fall of man in the Garden of Eden, but the new-man has come into existence only since the Church Age.

# The Holy Spirit in the Old Testament

A bogus attempt might be made to place the new-man back in the Age of Israel based upon enduement of Holy Spirit power on certain Old Testament personalities who were executing a divine purpose associated with *service*. This is an apples-and-oranges argument in the following sense. This argument fails to distinguish *character* from a service being performed. While supernatural power was occasionally provided for *service* in the Age of Israel, the person executing *service* in the power of the Spirit was always executing the *service* from his own *character*. However, in the Church Age, the born-again Christian is required to execute Christian *service* while in the sphere of the Spirit from the *character* of Jesus Christ. This was never true in any dispensation prior to the Church Age. Compare the Age of Israel with the Church Age:

| **Dispensation** | **Age of Israel** | **Church Age** |
| --- | --- | --- |
| Holy Spirit | temporarily indwelt | permanently indwelt |
| Purpose | service | character |
| Character | one's own | Christ |
| Old-man | yes | yes |
| New-man | no | yes |

# Chapter 12

# Old-man New-man Terminology and Distinctions

If the born-again Church Age believer is going to understand the Christian way of life as it relates to the resolution of the angelic conflict, there is some terminology and distinctions with which he should familiarize himself.

## Old-man New-man Terminology

| OLD-MAN | NEW-MAN |
|---|---|
| sinful nature | Holy Spirit |
| old-man | new-man |
| old-man thinking | new-man thinking |
| old-man feelings | new-man feelings |
| old-man speech | new-man speech |
| old-man overt activity | new-man overt activity |
| old-man logic | new-man logic |

## Old-man Terminology Defined

>sinful nature: the influence that totally corrupts the old-man.
>old-man: the personification of the soul that is under the influence of the sinful nature.
>old-man-thinking: the corrupted old-man belief system.
>old-man-feelings: feelings generated by an old-man belief system.
>old-man-speech: speech generated by an old-man belief system.
>old-man overt activity: overt activity generated by an old-man belief system.
>old-man logic: old-man rationale used to personally justify old-man functions.
>old-man function: everything the old-man thinks, feels, says, does, and rationalizes.

# New-man Terminology Defined

Holy Spirit: the new-man influence.
new-man: the personification of the soul that is under the influence of the Holy Spirit.
new-man-thinking: thinking the way Jesus would think.
new-man-feelings: feeling the way Jesus would feel.
new-man-speech: saying what Jesus would say.
new-man overt activity: acting like Jesus would act.
new-man logic: reasoning like Jesus would reason.
new-man function: functioning like Jesus would think, feel, speak, do, and reason.

# Old-man New-man Distinctions

The old-man is created at physical birth.
The new-man is created at spiritual birth.
The unbeliever has only an old-man.
The believer has both an old-man and a new-man.
The unbeliever has no choice but to function from his old-man.
The believer has a choice to function from the old-man or new-man.
The old-man can function in the four divine institutions.
The new-man can function in the four divine institutions.
The old-man is associated with reformation.
The new-man is associated with transformation.
The old-man's influence is the sinful nature.
The new-man's influence is the Holy Spirit.
Old-man function is personal sins and human good.
New-man function is minus personal sins and human good.
The old-man lives in defeat; the new-man lives in victory.
The old-man is egocentric; the new-man is Christocentric.
The old man produces mental, verbal, and overt sins.
The new-man does not produce mental, verbal, and overt sins.
Old-man function can resemble new-man function.
New-man function may or may not resemble old-man function.

# Chapter 13

# Old-man New-man: Two Belief Systems

The goal of the Christian way of life is not to go to heaven; however, it should be the initial goal of the unbeliever. The real goal of the Christian way of life is to become exactly like Jesus Christ in His humanity, and to do so is a very reachable goal. It requires *experiential* victory over the world, the flesh, and the devil.

There are three categories of truth: the laws of divine establishment and the four divine institutions; the Gospel; and the royal family honor code. All three categories are under severe attack in the world today. As a result of what I refer to as "the five generation slide" away from the absolute truths of God's Holy Word, Christianity today, for the most part, has been reduced to a religion-a ritual without reality. It has been reduced to obedience to God from the source of the old-man, that is, obedience to God in the energy of the flesh. Approximately 90% plus of all of Christianity today preaches and teaches a false method of salvation. This means that slightly more than 9% have an accurate understanding of the true mechanics of salvation. In addition, less than 2% of the 9% understands the mechanics of spirituality in the Church Age. That's about eighteen out of every ten thousand persons who have an accurate understanding of the spiritual way of life offered to the human race through Christianity-and eighteen out of ten thousand may be an overestimate. If you don't think that that's serious, just take a look at the mess that the world is in today, and ask yourself if there might not be a connection between that mess and a general lack of understanding among Christians concerning what Christianity is really all about? We are here to resolve a spiritual battle between God the Father and Satan, and yet the larger portion of the Church has distorted the Gospel and the truths associated with the royal family honor code, two of the three categories of truth needed to resolve the angelic conflict. The Gospel has been distorted by presenting a works oriented approach to salvation, and obedience to the royal family honor code is called for without ever telling Christians *how-to* perform what they are being told to do. Finally, personal freedom as the last bastion of truth is being plundered by government legislation. Is it any wonder that God the Father is ratcheting up the pressure of divine discipline and people are suffering for their blatant mishandling of God's plan for the human race?

In view of these introductory thoughts, I offer you the following information.

# Two Systems of Thinking in the World Today

1. There is an old-man belief system, an old-man way of thinking. These are synonymous terms.
2. There is a new-man belief system, a new-man way of thinking. These are synonymous terms.

Regarding these two systems of thinking, I believe the following statements to be true:

1. Every human being has a sinful nature, an old-man, and an old-man system of thinking, feeling, speaking, acting, and rationalizing.
2. Old-man function is what the old-man thinks, feels, says, does or reasons as he makes applications to the circumstances of life while yielded to the sinful nature. Here are some examples. In any circumstance of life, the old-man can become angry (mental-attitude sin), lie (verbal sin), drown himself in alcohol (overt sin). Anger, lying, and drunkenness are old-man functions as old-man reactions to circumstances of life.
3. Old-man logic is the old-man's rationale used to justify to himself that what he has thought, felt, said, or done is right, okay for him, in any circumstance of life. He says, "I was angry because . . . I lied because . . . I got drunk because. . ." and it's what follows the because that forms the logic that he uses to justify his old-man thought, feeling, speech, or action.
4. Every born-again Christian has a new nature, a new-man, the *availability* of new-man thinking, the *availability* of new-man feelings, the *availability* of new-man speech, the *availability* of new-man actions, and the *availability* of new-man logic. However, just because every Christian has a new-man living inside him doesn't mean that he will ever access that new-man. He may fail to access his new-man for one of several reasons:

He is never taught that he has a new-man.
Or, he is never taught HOW-TO access the new-man that he knows he has.
Or, he may believe he is actually accessing his new-man when in fact he isn't.
Or, he may misinterpret Romans 6:6, 11, and 13 so as to negate this passage as containing the true mechanics of accessing his new-man. Let me be specific here. If the word "yield" in Romans 6:13 is interpreted to mean confession of sin in 1 John 1:9, the new-man will never be accessed until the Holy Spirit is permitted to clarify this misunderstanding.

5. New-man *function* is what the new-man thinks, feels, says, does or reasons as he makes application to the circumstances of life while yielded to the indwelling Holy Spirit at the fourth step in "Operation KRRY:" first: know, second: reckon, third: reckon, and fourth: YIELD.
6. New-man *logic* is the new-man's rationale that he uses to justify his thoughts, feelings, speech, and actions associated with the circumstances of life.
7. Note that sinful nature and old-man are not synonymous terms. They are two sides of the same coin. You can't have one without the other. Where the old-man is, there you have the sinful nature, and where you have the sinful nature, there you have the old-man.
8. The sinful nature is the factor in every human being that corrupts everything the human being thinks, feels, says, does, or reasons after physical birth.
9. The sinful nature provides the *influence* that totally corrupts every aspect of old-man *function*.
10. The indwelling Holy Spirit provides the *influence* that perfects every aspect of new-man *function*.

    The purpose for what I am about to say is not meant as disagreement for the sake of disagreement, nor is it meant to be confrontational simply for the purpose of confrontation. It's simply a matter of my understanding.

# My View of Things the Way I Believe Them to Be

Today, most Christian denominations and most Christian organizations are religious in nature, works-oriented regarding how to become born-again, and legalistic regarding the moment-by-moment Christian walk. The works that they require for salvation are dead works produced by *default* yieldedness to the sinful nature. Application of corrupted old-man thinking produces corrupted old-man function that is rejected by the absolute righteousness of God.

Today, "religious" denominations and organizations call Christians to "obedience," but there is something inescapably wrong about their message. Obedience, when produced their way, is always from the source of the old-man because they never teach their followers how to access their new-man so that obedience can be accomplished from the source of their new-man. Here's a principle of life: Except for the application of the laws of divine establishment and the four divine institutions, anything accomplished from the source of the old-man is repugnant to God, no matter how well-intentioned the persons are who are producing the obedience. They may be doing the right thing, but they are doing it in the wrong way. They are doing the WHAT without the HOW.

If a Christian does not learn the mechanics (the how to) of accessing his new-man for new-man function, the bema seat experience will not be a pretty picture for that individual. Whatever good he has accomplished as a born-again Christian will be human good that will burn up as wood, hay, and stubble (1 Corinthians 3:12, 15). The result will be to suffer loss of distributable reward that has been provided and held for the believer since eternity past.

I respectfully ask this question. Regarding how some Christians view the old-man and the new-man concepts, where, when, and how do we incorporate know, reckon, reckon, yield, and then do-the-truth into our teaching and witnessing? To demonstrate the shallowness of some opposition to "Operation KRRY," I have been told that the "know, reckon, reckon, and yield" terminology comes from the King James Version, and if I would only use another Bible version the terminology would be different. My response: "Well, HELLO!! That's really deep, isn't it?"

What is an old-man belief system or old-man thinking? These synonymous terms refer to a partial or total distortion of any concept associated with the three categories of truth: 1) the laws of divine establishment and the four divine institutions, 2) the Gospel, and 3) the royal family honor code. Remember, evil is defined as any distortion of truth, no matter how slight the distortion.

If a fellow Christian is willing to acknowledge the existence of both an old-man belief system and a new-man belief system, he can be led to *understand* what the CONTENT of his new-man belief system *should be*, but until he is taught and learns *how-to* access his new-man that enables him to apply his new-man belief system, he will struggle to apply because his application will come from the source of his old-man. He will live in constant *defeat* by doing the things he shouldn't do, and not doing the things that he should do (Romans 7:15).

Any victory achieved by old-man function in the Church Age is spiritually worthless because it is achieved in the energy of the flesh. For example, an alcoholic claims victory by overcoming his alcoholism through function in a twelve-step-program; however, the benefit derived from his victory will be temporal in nature, but it has no eternal value.

The focus of an old-man belief system is "what," not "how." The focus of a new-man belief system is "what" and "how." I believe that a spiritually disastrous switch is taking place today in some arenas of teaching, preaching, counseling, and witnessing. The "what" is being taught as the "how." It's so subtle, but none-the-less disastrous. Here's how it occurs. Suppose that I say to someone, "I have a problem," and then explain the nature of my problem. Then I ask, "HOW do I get victory over this problem?" I have asked "how" do I get victory, but my counselor interprets my request as "what" am I to do to get victory over my problem. He then gives me the "what"-pray, give, go, stop, start, etc. The one seeking help has asked "how" to become victorious, but received the "what." The counselor believes that the "what" IS the "how." The one seeking counsel then goes on to even more failure because the "what-without-the-how" is failure waiting to occur. The real "how-to" is Romans 6:6, 6:11, 6:13 (know, reckon, reckon, yield)-and THEN do-the-truth-pray, give, go, stop, start, etc.

If Romans 6:6, 6:11, and 6:13 don't function in transition from the old-man belief system to the new-man belief system, the end result is a futile attempt to *reform* the old-man by doing what the new-man is supposed to be doing. This is energy of the flesh function. It is default yieldedness to the sin nature. Here's another principle. Old-man function is the *default* function when an application of Romans 6:6, 6:11, and 6:13 is by-passed, whether it is by-passed with or without cognizance.

Romans 6:6 says "knowing [present, active, participle of γινωσκω (ginosko)] this, that our old man WAS crucified [3$^{rd}$ person singular, aorist, passive, indicative of συσταυροω (sustauroo)] with Him, that the body of sin might be done away with, that we should no longer be slaves of sin." (NKJV)

    1. Concerning the word "knowing": You cannot apply what you don't know.
    2. If you don't know that your old-man WAS crucified with Christ, you are *defaulted* to old-man function.
    3. *Default* old-man function results in continual defeat in your battle against the world, the flesh, and the devil in the angelic conflict.

Colossians 3:8 says, "But now you yourselves are to put off [2nd person plural, aorist, passive, imperative of αποτιθημι (apotithemi)] all these: anger, wrath, malice, blasphemy, filthy language out of your mouth. 9 Don't lie to one another, since you have put off [nominative plural, aorist, middle, participle of απεκδυομαι (apekduomai)] the old man with his deeds, 10 and have put on [nominative plural, aorist, middle, participle of ενδυω (enduo)] the new man who is renewed in knowledge [new-man thinking] according to the image of Him who created him," (NKJV)

    1. From this verse, the following personal sins represent, but don't exhaust, old-man *function*: anger, wrath, malice [mental attitude sins], blasphemy, filthy language out of your mouth, lying to one another [sins-of-the-tongue].
    2. The following represent, but don't exhaust, pseudo-solutions and sinful reactions to the circumstances of life based upon an old-man belief system: anger, wrath, malice, blasphemy, filthy language out of your mouth, lying to one another.
    3. The phrase "since you HAVE put off the old man" indicates that the old-man has already been put-off. This occurred at the moment of salvation. God the Father identified the old-man WITH Christ on the cross. This can be referred to as retroactive positional death.
    4. This *judicial* death of the old-man is the basis for *experiential* victory whereby the Christian *experientially* puts-off anger, wrath, malice, blasphemy, filthy language out of your mouth, lying to one another, and every other form of mental, verbal, and overt personal sins.
    5. Since you have put off the old man with his deeds, the phrase "with his deeds" does not imply that you have already become

experientially victorious over the sins mentioned in this verse. It simply points out that the old-man is their source.

6. The new-man is put on at the moment of salvation, but is devoid of any new-man thinking (new-man belief system) until PERTINENT doctrine is internalized, moving it from the printed pages of the Bible to the soul's launching pad.

7. The fact that the new-man has been put on in this verse is simply an indication that you have been saved, i.e., born-again. Now, your new-man needs to be "renewed in knowledge according to the image of Him who created him."

8. I call your attention to the fact that Colossians 3:8 is one of those occasions wherein we as Christians are being told WHAT-TO-DO with no hint of HOW-TO do what we are being told to do. The HOW-TO is found in Romans 6:6, 6:11, 6:13 (know, reckon, reckon, and yield).

Ephesians 4:22 says, "That you put off [aorist, middle, infinitive of αποτιθημι (apotithemi)], concerning your former conduct, the old man which grows corrupt according to the deceitful lusts," (NKJV)

1. When you "put-off" the old-man, you "put-off" his conduct at the same time.
2. You kill the fruit (sinful conduct) by dealing with the root (sinful nature).

Ephesians 4:24 says, "And that you put on [aorist middle infinitive of ενδυω (enduo)] the new man which was created according to God, in true righteousness and holiness." (NKJV)

1. The phrase "put on the new-man" implies new-man function, that is, doing from the source of your new-man what Jesus would do in His humanity.
2. You already have the new-man. Now, learn to clothe him with true righteousness and holiness that is found in the truth of your new-man belief system.

# Section 5

# The Holy Spirit and the Christian Way of Life

# Chapter 14

# "In the Spirit"
εν πνευματι

## Introduction

The fourth step in "Operation KRRY" is yield-1) know, 2) reckon, 3) reckon, and 4) YIELD. When the Christian yields to God the Holy Spirit, he is said to be "in the Spirit." This phrase translates the preposition **εν** (en) + dative of the noun **πνευμα** (pneuma). This chapter will deal with what it means to be "in the Spirit."

According to Dan Wallace, "*Greek Grammar Beyond the Basics*," (p. 742), there are ten (10) different uses of the preposition **en** + dative. They are listed here in the order in which they appear in his book. (I have emboldened #1 to single out that form.):

1. **spatial/sphere: in (and various other translations)**
2. temporal: in, within, when, while, during
3. association: (often close personal relationship) with
4. cause: because of
5. instrumental: by, with
6. reference/respect: with respect to/with reference to
7. manner: with
8. things possessed: with (in the sense of *which possesses*)
9. standard: (equals a dative of rule): according to the standard of
10. as an equivalent for εις (eis) (with verbs of motion)

## "Greek" Magic?

There is nothing magic about the Greek language that leads to an accurate translation simply because something is written in Greek. In fact, by noting the different uses of the preposition **εν** (en) + dative, it should be obvious that if an accurate translation is to be consistent with God's intended meaning, an accurate interpretation must precede an accurate translation.

The following passages contain the phrase εν (en) + dative, translated "in the Spirit":

> Ephesians 6:18 Praying always with all prayer and supplication **in the spirit**, and watching thereunto with all perseverance and supplication for all saints; (KJV)

> Colossians 1:8 Who also declared unto us your love **in the spirit**. (KJV)

> Revelation 1:10 I was **in the spirit** on the Lord's day, and heard behind me a great voice, as of a trumpet, (KJV)

> Revelation 4:2 And immediately I was **in the spirit**: and, behold, a throne was set in heaven, and one sat on the throne. (KJV)

My interest is in the passages of Scripture where the sense of the passages would permit εν (en) + dative to be translated "in the Spirit" where "in the Spirit" would be interpreted as "spatial/sphere." Consider the "sphere" side of "spatial/sphere."

Please note that just because the English phrase "in the Spirit" appears multiple times in the same version of an English language Bible does not mean that each appearance should be interpreted in the same manner.

# The Use of εν (en) + Dative to Mean "Sphere"

1. Here's an assignment for you. Take paper and pencil and draw two circles.

circle #1: label "in the flesh"-sphere #1
circle #2: label "in the Spirit"-sphere #2

2. Consider that the born-again Christian at any given moment can be living his Christian life either in circle #1 or circle #2 with no other alternative. It's one sphere or the other.

3. Consider circles # 1 and #2 as absolutes. You are either in one circle or the other. The nature of these absolutes is that you cannot be in both circles at the same time.
4. Consider the fact that Romans 6:13 teaches you that the Christian can "yield" himself in either of two directions: 1) to his sinful nature; or 2) to God the Holy Spirit.

> Romans 6:13 Neither **yield** ye your members as instruments of unrighteousness unto sin [the sinful nature]: but **yield** yourselves unto God [the Holy Spirit], as those that are alive from the dead, and [ascensive use of the conjunction καί (kai) means even] your members as instruments of righteousness unto God. (KJV)

> The ascensive use of the conjunction καί (kai) simply means that when you **yield** *yourself* to God the Holy Spirit you are simultaneously **yielding** your *members* [body parts] in service to God the Father either from your priesthood or ambassadorship, whichever is applicable to the circumstance of life. You cannot yield yourself [total-self implied] without yielding your members [various body parts].

5. When the phrase "in the Spirit" is understood "spherically," the following would be true:

A. When you are "in the Spirit," all behavior will be "new-man" behavior.
B. When you are "in the Spirit," in-so-far-as your ***behavior*** is concerned, YOU are required to produce all the behavior whether it is mental, verbal, or overt. For example, the Christian, not the Holy Spirit, is required to produce the ninefold fruit of the Spirit: love, joy, peace, longsuffering, gentleness, goodness, faith, meekness, temperance: (Galatians 5:22-23 KJV)

   1) The Holy Spirit produces none of these.
   2) The born-again Christian must produce every one of these.

C. Why, then, are the characteristics of the humanity of Christ referred to as the "fruit of the Spirit?"

1)   It must be understood that any of the qualities listed as the ninefold fruit of the Spirit can be counterfeited by both an unbeliever and a carnal believer from the sphere "in the flesh."
2)   Hence, the question and the answer, "Why, then, are these characteristics of the humanity of Christ referred to as the fruit of the Spirit?" It's because they are to be produced by the believer while functioning "in the sphere of the Spirit."
3)   The phrase "fruit of the Spirit" answers the question WHERE you were you when you produced this fruit, not BY WHOM you produced it. You were "in the Spirit," not "in the flesh." It was you, not the Spirit, who produced it.
4)   This does not imply that if you were "in the Spirit" when you did these things that you could not have done the very same thing from the sphere of the flesh. It just so happens that you were "in the Spirit" when you did this, and not "in the flesh."

> a.   The point is this. When you manifest any one of what is referred to as a "fruit of the Spirit," both the old-man and the new-man can produce love, joy, peace, longsuffering, gentleness, goodness, faith, meekness, temperance. The old-man produces while "in the flesh," and the new-man produces while "in the Spirit." So, if someone says, "Where were you when you produced that?" your answer would be "in the flesh" or "in the Spirit."
> b.   The ninefold fruit of the Spirit in Galatians 5:22-23 is dealing with the question from "where" these fruit are to be produced, not "by whom" they are to be produced. You as a Christian will produce the fruit from the sphere to which you have yielded. Yieldedness (Romans 6:13) is the means by which a believer enters the realms of "in the Spirit" or "in the flesh."

5)   The new-man functions "in the sphere of the Spirit," and the old-man functions "in the sphere of the flesh." As far as Christians are concerned, the new-man is spiritual, and the old-man is carnal.
6)   It is the Christian who must produce love, produce peace, produce longsuffering, produce gentleness, produce goodness, produce faith, produce meekness, and produce temperance.

7) When the Christian produces the fruit from "within the sphere of the Spirit," the Christian is reproducing the character of Christ's humanity from which divinely good service emanates.

6. While Galatians 5:22-23 does not state that the ninefold fruit of the Spirit can be produced by a carnal believer and an unbeliever, they can do so none-the-less. Here's the difference. The carnal believer and the unbeliever produce from within the sphere of the flesh, and the spiritual Christian produces from within the sphere of the Spirit.
7. How does a believer get "in the Spirit" or "in the flesh?" It takes a mental attitude of surrender in one direction or the other. This is what is referred to as "yielding." When you yield, you surrender. The new-man yields to the sphere of the Spirit. The old-man yields to the sphere of the flesh.

# Displacement, Absorption, Infusion, and Organic Connection

These four terms are important to an accurate understanding of the relationship between the believer and the Holy Spirit. Being "in the Spirit" is best understood as absorption rather than displacement. When a solid rock is dropped into a tub full of water, the rock does not absorb the water. It displaces water. If you drop a towel into a tub full of water, the towel does not displace the water, it absorbs the water. In like manner, when the born-again Christian yields to the Holy Spirit and enters "the sphere of the Spirit," the Christian does not displace the Spirit, but absorbs the Spirit. As the towel absorbs the water, the water completely infuses the towel-not a dry spot on it. In like manner, when the believer is "in the Spirit," the believer passively absorbs the Spirit, and the Spirit passively infuses the believer. Absorption and infusion result in *organic connection.*

Dan Wallace uses the phrase *organic connection* on p. 129, "since believers are said to be in Christ, because of their *organic connection* to Him, they now associate with Him in many and profound ways."

The term "organic" indicates interrelationship. "Organic connection" describes *oneness,* and this type of oneness occurs in each of the following relationships: an unbeliever and his sinful nature are organically connected; a believer and his sinful nature are organically connected; and a believer and the Holy Spirit are organically connected.

This *oneness* will be illustrated analogously in the section below titled *In the Spirit Analogies*.

## Organic Connection and the Divine Decrees

"Organic connection" is the result of absorption and infusion. The concept of organic connection is a decree of God the Father. He decreed that when a post-canon Church Age believer functioning in "Operation KRRY" yields to God the Holy Spirit, the Spirit will be passively absorbed by the believer and the believer will be passively infused with the Spirit.

So, if someone were to ask the question, "Why does it work this way?" the answer is simple. God the Father decreed in eternity past that absorption and infusion will occur the moment the believer yields to God the Holy Spirit as the fourth step in "Operation KRRY."

## Summary Conclusion

"In the Spirit" is the sphere from within which the believer is to live his Christian life. This sphere is entered by yieldedness as a free-will choice in the fourth step of "Operation KRRY." From within the sphere of the Spirit, the believer functions from his new-man to produce Christ-like character and Christ-like service that is blessable in time and rewardable in eternity.

# Chapter 15

# "In the Spirit" Analogies and Demonstrations

## Introduction

This chapter is designed to demonstrate two analogies to assist in understanding the concept "in the spirit." It will also provide a demonstration of the concepts of *absorption* and *infusion*.

    The Christian produces thought, feeling, speech, acts (deeds), and rationales. Thought, feeling, speech, acts, and rationales are not the Christian, but manifestations produced by the Christian. When the Christian yields to the Holy Spirit in the fourth step in "Operation KRRY," the Christian can be said to be "in the Spirit." The Christian is not the Spirit, and the Spirit is not the Christian.

    When the Christian is "in the Spirit," the product of the union of the Christian and the Spirit is called the "new-man" and his manifestations are thought, feeling, speech, action, and rationalization.

## Two Analogies

    Two analogies will be presented that picture aspects of the union between the Christian and the Spirit. Why only aspects of the union? It's because analogies have a tendency to breakdown if the analogy is pressed too far. For example, if in the biblical analogy, the "fig tree" represents Israel, don't ask yourself what the bark on the fig-tree represents. It represents nothing in the analogy, and to think that it does presses the analogy beyond its intended meaning. So, the following analogies should not be pressed beyond the purpose for which they are intended.

### Analogy #1

    Analogy #1 is intended only to show the *nature of the union* between the Christian and the Spirit when the Christian is "in the Spirit."

Hydrogen (H) and oxygen (O) are distinctly different gases. However, when hydrogen and oxygen are combined, they form water ($H_2O$), a product completely different from hydrogen, a product completely different from oxygen, yet a combination of the two. If we establish (H) to represent the Christian, and (O) to represent the Holy Spirit, when the two gases are combined to make water, the water represents the new-man. The new-man is not the Christian, nor is the new-man the Holy Spirit, yet the new-man is a combination of both. (Isn't God wonderful? Hydrogen is a gas. Oxygen is a gas. However, hydrogen and oxygen, when combined, become a liquid. Water is a liquid. Liquid water is not a gas, but a combination of two gasses. The new-man is not the Christian. The new-man is not the Spirit; yet, the new-man is the personification of the union of the Christian and the Spirit. Is God amazing, or what!

## Analogy #2

Analogy #2 is intended only to show the *nature of the union* of the Christian and the Spirit when the Christian is "in the Spirit." Sodium (Na) and chloride (Cl) are elements different from one another. However, when they are combined, they become an ionic compound, NaCl (sodium chloride), that we know as salt. Salt is different from sodium, and salt is different from chloride; yet salt is a combination of both sodium and chloride. If we establish sodium (Na) to represent the Christian, and chloride (Cl) to represent the Holy Spirit, when the two elements are combined to form salt, the salt represents the new-man. The new-man is not the Christian, nor is the new-man the Holy Spirit; yet the new-man is a combination of both.

Please note that in these two analogies, the Holy Spirit is *passively* present in both. By yielding to the Spirit, the Christian is said to be "in the Spirit." When the Christian is "in the Spirit," the Christian is *infused* with the Spirit and the Spirit is *absorbed* by the Christian in such a manner that every thought, feeling, speech, action, and rationale produced by the Christian is manifested as divine character or divine service.

# Three Demonstrations

These demonstrations are designed to show how Christian thought, Christian feeling, Christian speech, Christian action, and Christian rationalization take on *divine nature* when they are manifested while the Christian is "in the Spirit." These demonstrations contain three props:

shamwow, dye, and water. Please, keep these three things separated in your mind.

Take three pieces of shamwow. Take three different colors of dye: red, blue, and green. Use three separate bowls each containing a pre-measured amount of water. The amount of water in each bowl is determined by the amount of water needed to completely soak a shamwow and leave no remaining water in the bowl when the shamwow is placed in the bowl.

Note carefully that the shamwows are not the dyes, the dyes are not the shamwows, and the shamwows and dyes are not the water. They are three separate phenomena: shamwows, dyes, and water.

Let the red dye represent Christian thought. Let the blue dye represent Christian speech. Let the green dye represent Christian deeds. Cover one shamwow with red dye, one with blue dye, and one with green dye. Each shamwow represents you as a born-again Christian. The shamwow and the red dye represent you and your thinking. The shamwow and blue dye represent you and your speech. The shamwow and the green dye represent you and your overt actions. Place the predetermined amount of water in three bowls, and let the water in each represent the Holy Spirit. Wringing-out the dye covered shamwows soaked with water will represent the Christian producing thought, speech, and action while "in the Spirit."

## Demonstration #1

Now, immerse the shamwow covered with red dye in bowl #1. This immersion is analogous to the Christian yielding to the Holy Spirit. The red shamwow absorbs the water and the water infuses the red shamwow. The red shamwow and the water are now organically connected. When the red shamwow is wrung-out, red water comes forth. The water is not red dye, and the red dye is not water, yet when the red shamwow is wrung-out, the water is red because of the organic connection between the shamwow and the water. When the Christian produces thought while yielded to the Spirit, the thought becomes divine in nature because of the organic connection between the believer and the Spirit.

## Demonstration #2

Now, immerse the shamwow covered with blue dye in bowl #2. This immersion is analogous to the Christian yielding to the Holy Spirit. The blue shamwow absorbs the water and the water infuses the blue shamwow. The blue shamwow and the water are now organically connected. When the blue shamwow is wrung-out, blue water comes forth. The water is not blue dye, and the blue dye is not water, yet when the blue shamwow is wrung-out, the water is blue because of the organic connection between the shamwow and the water. When the Christian produces speech while yielded to the Spirit, the speech becomes divine in nature because of the organic connection between the believer and the Spirit.

## Demonstration #3

Now, immerse the shamwow covered with green dye in bowl #3. This immersion is analogous to the Christian yielding to the Holy Spirit. The green shamwow absorbs the water and the water infuses the green shamwow. The green shamwow and the water are now organically connected. When the green shamwow is wrung-out, green water comes forth. The water is not green dye, and the green dye is not water, yet when the green shamwow is wrung-out, the water is green because of the organic connection between the shamwow and the water. When the Christian produces actions while yielded to the Spirit, the actions become divine in nature because of the organic connection between the believer and the Spirit.

## Demonstrations Continued

You can continue this demonstration by using two more shamwows and two more different colors of dye. Repeat the process, each shamwow representing you as the believer, with the two different colors of dye representing feeling and rationalization.

## Demonstrating Sinful Nature Influence

Instead of placing clear water representing the Holy Spirit in the bowls, place black dye in the water in each bowl. The water with black dye represents the influence of the sinful nature. Now, when you place the shamwows in the black water, and wring them out, the red dye, blue dye, and green dye are tainted with black dye indicating the organic connection between the believer and his sinful nature that influences thought, speech, and actions when the believer is yielded to his sinful nature.

# The Hungry-Heart

If someone should say, "This is much too deep, far over my head, too difficult to understand," that person has not yet been totally prepared to make sense of the spiritual life provided by God the Father. He will continue to process this life through the circumstances of life until such a heart-hunger exists that no matter how difficult the process of understanding seems to be, the hungry-heart will not cease to seek this wisdom until it becomes a reality of life. Heart-hunger increases in each of us as we finally figure out that our plan isn't working. Just how hungry is your heart?

# Chapter 16

# The Fruit of the Spirit
καρπος του πνευματος

**Text.** Galatians 5:22 But the fruit of the Spirit is love, joy, peace, longsuffering, gentleness, goodness, faith, 23 Meekness, temperance: against such there is no law. (KJV)

The word "fruit" (καρπος) is a nominative singular noun. The words "of the Spirit" (του πνευματος) are genitive singulars of the definite article ὁ and the noun πνευμα. The question arises regarding the type of genitive of the phrase ὁ πνευμα (the Spirit).

According to Dan Wallace, "*Greek Grammar Beyond the Basics*," (pp. 727-729) there are thirty three possible uses of the genitive case. Well, now, one might scratch his head and say, "Wow! I wonder which use is intended in Galatians 5:22?"

I believe that many Christians view the phrase "of the Spirit" as a "genitive of production/producer" wherein the genitive noun (Spirit) produces the noun (fruit) to which it stands related. In other words, the fruit is produced *by* the Spirit. While this may be a common understanding, I believe it to be incorrect. My belief is not based solely upon an exegetical study of the subject "in the Spirit," but also upon forty-eight years of Christian living wherein I cannot say that I am aware of the Holy Spirit producing one bit of Christ-like behavior in me that I did not produce myself. Blasphemous? No. Biblically correct? Yes. I am not leaving the Holy Spirit out of the process. It's simply that His role is passive, rather than active as is commonly taught and believed.

Dan Wallace lists the phrase "of the Spirit" under genitive of production/producer, but does so as a footnote in the section titled "Illustrations (possible)" along with five other references, two of which are followed by (perhaps). Perhaps? This certainly isn't a strong case for genitive of production/producer. In fact, on p. 104, Wallace says of the genitive of production/producer, "This usage of the genitive is not common."

It's the "genitive of association" that explains the meaning of the phrase "of the Spirit." It says that the genitive substantive (Spirit) indicates the one with whom the noun to which it stands related (fruit) is associated.

This means that while the "Spirit" is associated with the "fruit," the Spirit is not producing the fruit.

Regarding the genitive of association, Wallace states, "This usage is somewhat common, but only in certain collocations," and that "fruit of the Spirit" does not represent a collocation. If on this basis, someone were to argue for "genitive of production/producer" against the "genitive of association," the antagonist should be told, "Read on, brother." In his notes on p. 129 when discussing Matthew 23:30, Wallace states "This is one of the less frequent examples involving a head noun/adjective (fruit) not prefixed by συν (sun). The point: "fruit of the Spirit" can be a genitive of association without the head noun (fruit: karpoj) containing the prefix συν (sun) meaning "with." Whether anyone believes that "fruit of the Spirit" is a genitive of association or not, it is clear, that there is no grammatical reason for denying its possibility.

## Concluding Statement

I believe that "fruit of the Spirit" in Galatians 5:22 is a genitive of association making this understanding consistent with the dative of sphere "in the Spirit" in Ephesians 5:18. While the Christian is producing the fruit of Christ-likeness, he is doing so because he is associated with the Holy Spirit (Galatians 5:22) through yieldedness (Romans 6:13) to the Holy Spirit which places him in the sphere of the Spirit (Ephesians 5:18).

# Chapter 17

# Who Produces the Ninefold Fruit of the Spirit?

Galatians 5:22 But the fruit of the Spirit is love, joy, peace, longsuffering, gentleness, goodness, faith, 23 Meekness, temperance: against such there is no law. (KJV)

## Introduction

The ninefold fruit of the Spirit is stated to be the fruit of the Spirit. It is not the fruit of someone or something else. It is specifically stated to be the fruit of the Spirit. There should be no doubt that the word Spirit refers to the Holy Spirit.

Because the fruit of the Spirit is said to be the fruit of the Spirit, a common perception is that this means that the Holy Spirit produces this fruit. This perception is based upon the belief that the phrase "of the Spirit" in Galatians 5:22 is a genitive of producer/production and is reinforced by the belief that "with the Spirit" in Ephesians 5:18 is a dative of instrumentality. If the Holy Spirit actually produces this fruit, an honest question might be this. What is meant by produces? Does the Holy Spirit manufacture this fruit without any believer participation? You know, something like, "Look fellow, just get out of the way and I'll handle this." When Christians are taught that the Holy Spirit produces the ninefold fruit, they generally draw the conclusion that they have no responsibility in spiritual fruit production. If the believer knows which of the ninefold fruit needs to be manifested, does he just trust that somehow or another the Holy Spirit will magically or supernaturally produce that specific fruit, and BANG!-there it is! WOW! That's easy. Yes, and wouldn't it be if that's how it worked? Experientially, manifestation failure after failure discloses the fact that it doesn't work that way. If it did, every time failure occurred the believer could turn to God the Father-remember, it's His plan-and say, "See, the Holy Spirit has failed again. I wanted to manifest the fruit required by my circumstance, but the Holy Spirit didn't come through." This dialogue is not necessary because the plan doesn't work that way.

Consider the following truths regarding the Holy Spirit: 1) He is the third Person of the Godhead; 2) His responsibility in the Father's plan is to reveal the plan and restore to the plan those who are separated from it; 3) He indwells every born-again Christian; 4) He indwells the believer's human spirit; 5) He is omnipotent; and 6) He does have a role in the believer's manifestation of the ninefold fruit of the Spirit.

**Thesis.** In any given circumstance that requires a believer to *manifest* one or more of the ninefold fruit of the Spirit, it's the believer's responsibility to *produce* the specific fruit. It's NOT the Holy Spirit's responsibility to *produce* the specific fruit as is commonly believed.

If a believer's circumstance requires the manifestation of a fruit of the Spirit, a decision must be made regarding the specific fruit to apply. Can you imagine needing to apply agape love, but applying joy instead? Can you imagine needing to apply temperance (self-control), but applying faith instead?

Someone might ask, "Well, what's wrong with applying joy or faith to any circumstance if they're part of the ninefold fruit of the Spirit?" As honest as that question might be, the problem is that joy isn't agape love and faith isn't temperance. If you need agape love, you need agape love, not joy. If you need temperance, you need temperance, not faith.

Consider this illustration. If I need to repair a flat tire on my automobile, will filling my gas tank with gas fix the flat tire? The answer is no because a flat tire is not repaired by filling the gas tank. As beneficial as it might be to fill the gas tank with gas, filling the gas tank will not fix a flat tire. In the same manner, applying joy won't work when agape love is needed; and applying faith won't work when temperance is needed.

The believer must understand that the ninefold fruit of the Spirit are not fruit of the Spirit because the Spirit is producing the fruit, but because the believer is functioning from the source of his new-man in association with the Spirit through yieldedness. This same ninefold fruit can be manifested by the old-man as "fruit of the flesh" if the believer is yielded to the sinful nature. While these ninefold fruit are never mentioned in Scripture as "fruit of the flesh," it doesn't take but a brief look at each of these fruit to realize that every one of them can be produced while functioning from the source of the old-man. It doesn't need to be stated anywhere for it to be so. Just stop long enough to think.

The new-man in every born-again Christian can be accessed only when the following conditions are met: 1) salvation is the first requirement; 2) the believer must then be clean before the Lord through the confession of any unconfessed post-salvation sins; 3) the believer must then function in "Operation KRRY"; 4) the believer must then produce the specific fruit of the Spirit needed for the circumstance. Note that it's the believer who must produce the specific fruit. This means that the Holy Spirit is NOT the One who does the producing. What then is the role of the Holy Spirit in the production of ANY of the ninefold fruit of the Spirit? Let's explore His role.

The Holy Sprit's role does not become an issue until the believer is functioning in the sphere of the Spirit. By actualizing (applying) "Operation KRRY," an organic connection occurs between the believer and the Spirit. The Spirit is passively absorbed and the believer is passively infused. Now, every fruit initiated by the believer is infused with the divine nature of the Spirit. The role of the Spirit in the manifestations of the ninefold fruit is one of passive infusion. He passively infuses everything produced by the believer's new-man. The net result is the divine character of Christ manifested every time the believer produces fruit that has been infused with the Spirit's divine nature. Without the Spirit's involvement, whatever fruit might be manifested is a manifestation of an old-man function.

Many Christians do not realize or are not willing to admit that even an unbeliever and a carnal believer can manifest any one of the ninefold fruit. Both can manifest love, joy, peace, longsuffering, gentleness, goodness, faith, meekness, and temperance (self-control). While this thought might be unpopular, it's nonetheless true. Its unpopularity is based upon the false assumption that the Holy Spirit *produces* the ninefold fruit of the Spirit. Since the unbeliever is NOT indwelt with the Holy Spirit, the conclusion is that it's impossible for the unbeliever to produce this fruit. Although the carnal believer is indwelt with the Spirit, carnality results in broken fellowship with the Spirit; therefore, the assumption is that the carnal believer could not possibly produce this fruit. Both assumptions are incorrect. Both the unbeliever and the carnal believer can produce these fruit, but they produce from the sphere of the flesh which is old-man production.

Caution! Words are important. Note that the unbeliever and the carnal believer are said to produce fruit, but not fruit of the spirit. While it's possible for them to produce exactly the same fruit from the source of the old-man as is produced from the source of the new-man, it can only be said that they are producing fruit, but not the fruit of the Spirit. Do not include the phrase "of the Spirit" when talking about unbeliever and carnal believer's production. Fruit, yes; but fruit of the Spirit, no.

# Summary

The Holy Spirit does NOT *produce* the ninefold fruit of the Spirit as is perceived by some. His role is to passively infuse the believer's offerings with His divine nature. The net result is that the believer produces fruit that manifests the character of the humanity of Jesus Christ from within the sphere of the Spirit.

# Thesis Conclusion

In any given circumstance that requires a believer to manifest one or more of the ninefold fruit of the Spirit, it is the believer's responsibility to produce the specific fruit. It's the believer's responsibility to produce love, joy, peace, longsuffering, gentleness, goodness, faith, meekness, and temperance. The Holy Spirit plays the passive role of infusing the believer's offerings with divine nature. It's this cooperative effort between believer and Spirit that results in the character of Jesus Christ being manifested in a life situation.

While the theological position that the Holy Spirit does not produce the fruit of the Spirit may run contrary to the common perception among Christians, it places the responsibility right where it belongs. The Christian is responsible to produce the fruit of the Spirit that manifests Christ-likeness.

# How Can I Tell?

If someone asks, "If an unbeliever, a carnal believer, and a spiritual believer can all three produce the ninefold fruit-notice that I didn't say ninefold fruit of the Spirit-how can I tell whether the one producing the fruit is an unbeliever, a carnal believer, or a spiritual believer?" The answer is that under certain conditions it may be humanly impossible to make that determination. The interesting thing is that God the Father, whose plan it is, has not assigned that responsibility to any of us. It is he who knows, and that's what's important. Remember, every decision made by every human being is made in relationship to the resolution of the angelic conflict; and every time an unbeliever or carnal believer produce one of the ninefold fruit, an omniscient God the Father is not fooled by the manifestation because He knows the fleshly source of that production. Isn't it interesting that if the fruit produced by the unbeliever or carnal believer is directed toward another human being, the one toward whom the fruit is directed is an immediate benefactor of the manifestation, but there is no eternal benefit for the unbeliever or carnal believer doing the producing. However, the same omniscient God is able to distinguish a spiritual believer from a carnal believer and an unbeliever; so, when the spiritual believer produces one of the nine fold fruit, not only does the one toward whom the fruit is manifested benefit temporally, eternal benefit is accrued by the spiritual believer who is producing the fruit.

# Chapter 18

# The Seven Manifestations of the Spirit

## Introduction

As a young pastor, I learned from older pastors and often taught what they taught. I trusted them because their thoughts appeared to be deeper than what I understood at the time. Basically, I followed a denominational line of thought, and I am indebted to those from whom I initially learned because of the solid foundation that was laid upon which I could build.

As the process of spiritual growth takes place in a Christian's life, more often that not, some things previously believed require refinement. Sometimes it's necessary to abandon a thought and replace it with a new one. However, it's not necessary to go on a guilt trip because you might have misunderstood or even taught something that had not yet been completely refined in your own thinking. No guilt trips!

What follows is not an excuse, but a reason. As the five generation slide engulfed this nation, most young men gifted with the gift of pastor-teacher, without realizing it themselves at the time, were without sound doctrinal mentors or academic institutions capable of clearly articulating the decreed mechanics of the spiritual life demanded by God the Father. It was possible to be evangelistically strong while being weak in the moment-by-moment walk. The net result is that young pastors have had to learn the hard way, just like everyone else. However, there is one major difference that distinguishes the gifted pastor-teacher from those who do not possess this gift. The spiritual gift provides an intrinsic passion to know the truth. That passion drives them to its discovery-sooner or later-most often later rather than sooner.

Coming to know the absolute truth on any subject does not always come instantaneously. It often develops, passing from refinement to refinement as additional information is learned. Refinement clarifies understanding. There's danger in believing that some level of refinement reached is the last word on a subject prior to the time that the complete truth has actually been learned. Is it possible to have the final word on a given subject? I think the answer is yes.

Unless there has been some malevolent motivation behind a pastor-teacher's teaching, the disciples who learn from him should be thankful to God for whatever they have learned because it becomes the basis for the next level of understanding if a refinement becomes necessary. The old-man in all of us would rather say, "That scoundrel has misled me, and look at all the time I've wasted listening to him." Question: Where would you be if you hadn't already been brought to your present level of understanding by that pastor-teacher?

It must be understood that whatever a pastor-teacher believes and teaches, his thoughts represent his paradigm at that moment. If he determines that his understanding needs to be refined, any refinement will affect his present paradigm. As he tweaks his paradigm, this may result in the need to readjust his understanding of other concepts previously taught. This is true about my teaching on the subject of the seven manifestations of the Spirit. I have made major adjustments to what I previously believed and taught on this subject.

What caused my paradigm shift on the subject of the seven manifestations of the Spirit? My understanding of Ephesians 5:18 was the problem. Early in my Christian life, I believed that I was commanded to be filled WITH the Holy Spirit. This led me into a "tongues" experience. As I grew to understand that all forms of tongues ceased in AD 70, I realized that my experience was spurious, and I ceased its practice. I was led to understand that Ephesians 5:18 didn't command me to be filled WITH the Spirit, but commanded the Christian to be filled BY MEANS OF the Spirit. My paradigm shifted from the Holy Spirit being poured into the Christian to the Holy Spirit being the One who was doing the pouring. The shift was from the Holy Spirit being the CONTENT poured to the Holy Spirit being the INSTRUMENT doing the pouring. Enter Galatians 5:22-23.

Now that the Holy Spirit is doing the pouring, I believed that this Galatians passage was teaching me that the Holy Spirit's responsibility was to produce in me what I was incapable of producing myself. In view of my refined understanding, this seemed reasonable to me. I kept telling myself, "Just give Him time; you'll finally see results." However, as time passed, I realized that both the quantity and quality of the fruit of the Spirit was still lacking in my life. This led me to revise my understanding in two areas: first, the phrase "fruit of the Spirit" in Galatians 5:22 previously thought to represent a "genitive of producer/production;" second, the phrase "filled with the Spirit" in Ephesians 5:18 previously thought to represent an "instrumental dative" of the word "Spirit." I now hold that "fruit of the Spirit" represents a "genitive of association," and "filled with the Spirit" represents a "dative of sphere." These two adjustments greatly affect what I have previously taught about the seven manifestations of the Spirit. My desire is to clarify my revised position.

## My Previous Teaching

Here, I list the seven manifestations of the Spirit as I previously taught them:

1. The H.S. produces Christian character. (Galatians 5:22-23)
2. The H.S. produces Christian service. (1 Corinthians 12:4)
3. The H.S. teaches. (John 16:12-15)
4. The H.S. promotes praise and thanksgiving. (Ephesians 5:18ff)
5. The H.S. leads. (Romans 8:14; Galatians 5:18)
6. The Holy Spirit witnesses with our spirit. (Romans 8:16)
7. The H.S. intercedes. (Romans 8:26)

In each of the seven manifestations listed above, the role of the Holy Spirit is viewed as ACTIVE. He is the One who is directly producing everything. He is said to *produce* Christian character; He is said to *produce* Christian service; He is the One doing the teaching; He is the One *promoting* praise and thanksgiving; He is the One *leading;* He is the One *witnessing;* and He is the One *interceding.*

The immediate question is this. If the Holy Spirit has an ACTIVE role in each of these seven manifestations, what is the role of the born-again Christian in each manifestation? Regardless of your answer, we must intellectually concede that if the Spirit's role is ACTIVE, the born-again Christian can have only one of three possible roles: 1) none; 2) passive; or 3) active in cooperation with the Spirit.

## A Basic Assumption

Unless otherwise stated, everything beyond this point assumes that the born-again Christian is operating within the "sphere of the Spirit" disregarding whether the Spirit is actively or passively participating in a manifestation.

# Absorption and Infusion

The concepts of absorption and infusion are both *passive* in nature. The moment a born-again Christian yields to God the Holy Spirit at the fourth step of "Operation KRRY," that believer enters the "sphere of the Spirit." Instantaneously, the Holy Spirit *passively* infuses the believer and the believer *passively* absorbs the Holy Spirit. Absorption and infusion are complete at that moment. The believer has been totally infused, and the Spirit has been totally absorbed. The acts of *passive* absorption and *passive* infusion result in an organic connection between the believer and the Holy Spirit. Organic connection implies *oneness* of the believer and the Spirit. Remember, the processes of absorption and infusion are both *passive* in nature.

# Who Produces?

A question arises regarding the manifestations of Christian character and Christian service. Who produces the manifestations? Is it the born-again Christian or the Holy Spirit?

# Active or Passive Role?

Another question arises regarding the role of the born-again Christian and the role of the Holy Spirit in the production of Christian character and Christian service. Are their roles active or passive?

The difference between active and passive must be understood. Active implies an action required to produce a desired result. Passive implies being positioned in such a manner as to be drawn upon for the purpose of producing a desired result. Perhaps the concept of passive is more difficult to quickly understand. An example will be used to illustrate the Holy Spirit's passivity. If I want to nail two boards together, I will need a nail to do so. For the nail to be used, it doesn't have to do anything except be available. When I am ready to nail the boards together I pick up the nail, hit it with a hammer, and the boards are nailed together. Now that the boards are nailed together, I can't say that the nail did anything. I can only say that the nail was available for use to achieve a desired end.

When the Holy Spirit's role is passive, His role is the same as the nail. He is simply available to be drawn upon to achieve a desired end. When the believer is organically connected to the Spirit, the believer's every thought, feeling, spoken word, overt action, and rationale are infused with Holy Spirit nature. It's no wonder that under this condition God the Father's righteousness graciously accepts the believer's offerings from his priesthood or ambassadorship. They are divinely infused.

The believer's role is active in fruit production. It is produced from within the sphere of the Spirit. If the believer does not produce the fruit, no fruit will be produced.

# Two Questions Answered

In view of the phrase "of the Spirit" in Galatians 5:22 being a "genitive of association," and the phrase "with the Spirit" in Ephesians 5:18 being a "dative of sphere," two questions will now be answered.

Question #1: Who actually produces what has been referred to as the seven manifestations of the Spirit? Let's consider each manifestation separately.

1. Christian character: the born-again Christian produces the character.
2. Christian service: the born-again Christian produces service.
3. Teaching: the Holy Spirit produces the teaching.
4. Praise and thanksgiving: the born-again Christian produces praise and thanksgiving.
5. Leading/guiding: the Holy Spirit produces the leading/guiding.
6. Witness with our spirit: the Holy Spirit produces the witness.
7. Intercession: the Holy Spirit produces the intercession.

Question #2: Are the roles of the Holy Spirit and born-again Christian active or passive?

1. Christian character:
born-again Christian: active (function produced within the sphere of the Spirit)
Holy Spirit: passive (the sphere from within which believer's function occurs)
2. Christian service:
born-again Christian: active (function produced within the sphere of the Spirit)
Holy Spirit: passive (the sphere from within which believer's function occurs)

3. Teaching:
   born-again Christian: passive (received when the believer has met the conditions for internalization)
   Holy Spirit: active (produced when the believer has met the conditions for internalization)
4. Praise and thanksgiving:
   born-again Christian: active (function produced within the sphere of the Spirit)
   Holy Spirit: passive (the sphere from within which believer's function occurs)
5. Leading/guiding:
   born-again Christian: passive (received when the believer has met the conditions for internalization)
   Holy Spirit: active (produced when the believer has met the conditions for internalization)
6. Witnesses with our spirit:
   born-again Christian: passive (received when the believer has met the conditions for internalization)
   Holy Spirit: active (produced when the believer has met the conditions for internalization)
7. Intercession:
   born-again Christian: passive (received when the believer is in the sphere of the Spirit)
   Holy Spirit: active (produced while the believer has met the conditions for internalization)

# Conclusion

The seven manifestations of the Spirit are understood differently from my original teaching due to a clearer understanding of the "genitive of association" and "dative of sphere" in Galatians 5:22 and Ephesians 5:18 respectively.

I now understand and believe that the believer actively yields to God the Holy Spirit as the fourth step in "Operation KRRY" to enter the sphere of the Spirit where the believer is passively infused with the Spirit and the Spirit is passively absorbed by the believer from which organic connection the believer actively manifests the functions of his priesthood and ambassadorship.

This understanding places the responsibility squarely where it belongs. The believer is responsible to produce Christian function from the source of his new-man while operating in the sphere of the Spirit. This favorably impacts the resolution of the angelic conflict while simultaneously honoring and glorifying God the Father who decreed this marvelous plan.

# Section 6

# Agape Love and the Christian Way of Life

# Chapter 19

# Agape Love: What Is It?

The purpose of this chapter is to offer a definition of agape love, and to do so in such a manner as to be consistent with the Word of God. Among other things, I will attach my definition to the concepts of freedom and the angelic conflict. Without these attachments, I believe that when agape love is defined as unconditional love, this definition makes very little sense. I listened to that abbreviated definition for years, and finally said: "You're telling me that I need to unconditionally love (fill-in this blank with a name)," and then I asked, "Why?" The corresponding answer, "Because the Bible says you should." No. That's *where* I'm told to unconditionally love. That doesn't answer the question "why?" It was only after I had come to clearly understand the concepts of freedom and the angelic conflict that the meaning of agape love began to unfold and make sense to me.

Do not confuse my definition of agape love with its manifestations described in 1 Corinthians 13:4-7. My definition provides the meaning of the word. 1 Corinthians 13:4-7 identifies manifestations of agape love. This chapter focuses on its definition rather than its manifestations.

## Agape Love Defined

Agape love is an unemotional mental attitude of respect that recognizes another person's freedom to pursue his own internalized goal as long as the pursuit of that goal does not interrupt another person's right to pursue his own goal.

Agape love *respects* another person's inalienable right to *freely* make both good and bad decisions in the spiritual battle known as the angelic conflict.

## Agape Love and Freedom of Choice

Freedom of choice includes choices made before-the-fact and after-the-fact. Before-the-fact means that someone has not yet performed an act (good or bad), but the potential exists to do so. After-the-fact means that an act (good or bad) has already taken place. Until you grow spiritually, you'll find it easier to agape love the person who is only thinking about harming you. It's far more difficult to agape love the person who has already harmed you. However, an application of agape love is required in both cases-before-the-fact and after-the-fact.

# Freedom's Source and Environment

Freedom comes from God, not man.
Freedom is the environment in which agape love is designed to function.

# Agape Love Must Be Tied to Freedom

Agape love is correctly understood only when its function is tied to another person's freedom. If freedom is not understood and applied toward others, what is deemed to be agape love may not be agape love at all. If you think that you're directing agape love toward another person, your love is NOT agape love if you're NOT extending the inalienable right of freedom of choice to the person you say you're loving. The other person's freedom to choose is the key to recognizing whether your love is agape love or not.

# Agape Love and Irresponsible Freedom

Irresponsible freedom is defined as that form of freedom that seeks to achieve one's own internalized goals the pursuit of which disrupts another person's freedom to do the same. If an act of irresponsible freedom has an attending predetermined consequence, and it should, it is not inconsistent with agape love to recognize an irresponsible act and to follow it with the implementation of that consequence. "But where's your agape love for this violator?" someone might ask, looking for the consequence to be diminished or cancelled. That's the wrong question. The question should have been, "But what about the person who was injured when his inalienable right to responsibly pursue his own internalized goal was disrupted?" The implementation of consequence for a violation of freedom is not inconsistent with agape love if the consequence is implemented objectively. An illustration of a consequence implemented subjectively would be the parent who angrily implements the consequence. It's the parental anger that makes the implementation subjective.

## Agape Love and the Angelic Conflict

Negative choices manifested by fallen angels in eternity past offended the absolute righteousness of God the Father whose plan they had violated. When the righteousness of God is offended, His justice swings into action. Justice can either bless or curse. It blesses positive choices and curses negative choices. Satan's negative choices caused the justice of God to condemn him and every angel who followed after him. The condemnation was banishment into the lake of fire, tantamount to eternal separation from the God who authored creation. Remember, the Father's agape love permits negative decisions, but not without consequence. The decreed consequence of angelic negative choices toward God the Father's offer of angelic salvation is banishment to the lake of fire (Matthew 25:41) after the great white throne judgment (Revelation 20:11).

## Agape Love in the Church Age Described

As previously indicated, a distinction should be made between definition and description. A definition gives the meaning of a word. A description gives the conditions associated with a word. Agape love is defined as a mental attitude of respect expressed toward another person. Respect is truly manifested toward another person when it permits the one being loved to freely make decisions that are consistent with or contrary to God's will. Agape love is described (characterized) in 1 Corinthians 13:4-7 (NLT).

> Love is patient and kind.
> Love is not jealous or boastful or proud or rude.
> Love does not demand its own way.
> Love is not irritable.
> Love keeps no record of when it has been wronged.
> Love is never glad about injustice.
> Love rejoices whenever the truth wins out.
> Love never gives up.
> Love never loses faith.
> Love is always hopeful.

Love endures through every circumstance.

# Is Agape Love Sacrificial?

I have offered a definition of agape love. When my definition comes up in conversation, more often than not, the response is "Yes, but . . ." and the "but" is followed by a comment that agape love carries with it some form of "loving" action toward the one to whom agape love is being offered. The word sacrifice is frequently used by those who are somewhat uncomfortable with my definition because it doesn't include some sacrificial act rendered toward the recipient. The implication seems to be that agape love will always manifest itself toward the recipient in the form of doing something sacrificially for or giving something sacrificially to the recipient. This would *add* something to the recipient that was not possessed before the sacrificial act occurred. For example, if you don't have a coat and I give you mine, you benefit from something added to you that you didn't formerly possess. If, however, I withhold a slap to your face because you said something derogatory about me, I can't say that withholding the slap added anything to you. You are a benefactor only in the sense that I haven't done something to you. I respectfully reject the notion that if agape love is to be agape love it must do something sacrificially for the recipient that necessarily adds something to the recipient that was not possessed before agape love was offered. I am challenging the notion that agape love adds anything to its recipient based upon an examination of 1 Corinthians 13:4-7 that seems to be the Scripture most often appealed to when agape love is being discussed. The question is this. If agape love does something FOR its recipient that adds to the recipient, what is being ADDED in conjunction with the following fifteen words or phrases found in the 1 Corinthians 13 passage? I will use the New Living Translation only because of the modern English that it provides.

**patient**. Is this not a manifestation of RESPECT for another person's freedom to pursue his own internalized goal? Showing patience ADDS nothing to a recipient.

**kind**. Is this not a manifestation of RESPECT for another person's freedom to pursue his own internalized goal? Showing kindness ADDS nothing to a recipient.

**not boastful.** Is this not a manifestation of RESPECT for another person's freedom to pursue his own internalized goal? Not boastful ADDS nothing to a recipient.

**not proud.** Is this not a manifestation of RESPECT for another person's freedom to pursue his own internalized goal? Not proud ADDS nothing to a recipient.

**not rude.** Is this not a manifestation of RESPECT for another person's freedom to pursue his own internalized goal? Not rude ADDS nothing to a recipient.

**demand its own way.** Is this not a manifestation of RESPECT for another person's freedom to pursue his own internalized goal? Not demanding ADDS nothing to a recipient.

**not irritable.** Is this not a manifestation of RESPECT for another person's freedom to pursue his own internalized goal? Not irritable ADDS nothing to a recipient.

**keeps no record of when it has been wronged.** Is this not a manifestation of RESPECT for another person's freedom to pursue his own internalized goal? Keeping no record ADDS nothing to a recipient.

**never glad about injustice.** Is this not a manifestation of RESPECT for another person's freedom to pursue his own internalized goal? Never glad about injustice ADDS nothing to a recipient.

**rejoices whenever the truth wins out.** Is this not a manifestation of RESPECT for another person's freedom to pursue his own internalized goal? Rejoicing ADDS nothing to a recipient.

**never gives up.** Is this not a manifestation of RESPECT for another person's freedom to pursue his own internalized goal? Never gives up ADDS nothing to a recipient.

**never loses faith.** Is this not a manifestation of RESPECT for another person's freedom to pursue his own internalized goal? Never losing faith ADDS nothing to a recipient.

**always hopeful.** Is this not a manifestation of RESPECT for another person's freedom to pursue his own internalized goal? Always hopeful ADDS nothing to a recipient.

**endures through every circumstance.** Is this not a manifestation of RESPECT for another person's freedom to pursue his own internalized goal? Enduring through every circumstance ADDS nothing to a recipient.

Instead of agape love being viewed as "adding something to a recipient," all of these manifestations seem to be associated with "NOT doing something TO someone else." Are these not applications of my definition of agape love, that is, you showing RESPECT for another person's freedom to pursue an internalized goal in such a manner that you are not interrupting that person's freedom to do so?

Why then are there fifteen different conditions (manifestations, attributes) associated with agape love. It's because different circumstances require different responses. Agape love does not determine the response. Circumstance determines the response. Every circumstance of life has an appropriate new-man response. Possible responses are listed in 1 Corinthians 13:4-7. Agape love is the mental attitude from which the new-man response is made.

# Agape Love in Terms of Sacrifice

A brief look at each of the manifestations of agape love listed in 1 Corinthians 13:4-7 is considered in terms of sacrifice made and who it is that's making the sacrifice.

**patient.** patience sacrifices old-man freedom to be impatient.

**kind.** kindness sacrifices old-man freedom to be unkind.

**not boastful.** not boastful sacrifices old-man freedom to be boastful.

**not proud.** not proud sacrifices old-man freedom to be proud.

**not rude.** not rude sacrifices old-man freedom to be rude.

**does not demand its own way.** does not demand its own way sacrifices old-man freedom to demand one's own way.

**not irritable.** not irritable sacrifices old-man freedom to be irritable.

**keeps no record of when it has been wronged.** keeping no record sacrifices old-man freedom to keep record.

**never glad about injustice.** never glad about injustice sacrifices old-man freedom to be glad about injustice.

**rejoices whenever the truth wins out.** rejoicing when truth wins out sacrifices old-man freedom to not rejoice when truth wins out.

**never gives up.** never gives up sacrifices old-man freedom to give up.

**never loses faith.** never losing faith sacrifices old-man freedom to lose faith.

**always hopeful.** always hopeful sacrifices old-man freedom to never be hopeful.

**endures through every circumstance.** enduring every circumstance sacrifices old-man freedom to never endure any circumstance.

    A definition and a description are different from one another. A definition explains the meaning of word. A description sets forth the attributes of what has been defined. It is acknowledged that some definitions may be extended to include description, but definition is not description and description is not definition. 1 Corinthians 13:4-7 designates attributes, not definition.
    Is it possible to define agape love in four words or less? The answer is yes. LIVE AND LET LIVE!!

# Agape Love and Sacrificial Giving

    In view of the previous subsection, should we conclude that when a born-again Christian is manifesting agape love toward another person that the person manifesting the love will never give anything to a person in need? This conclusion would be equally as wrong as to believe that agape love will always give. Giving to someone is not determined by some rule found in the Bible that requires the Christian to legalistically do so. Giving is a matter of Holy Spirit leadership. Is He leading to give or not? If He is, give. If He isn't, don't. If you're led to give and you do, you're not giving because of agape love. You're giving because of Holy Spirit leadership. If you're not led to give, and you don't, it's not because you don't have agape love. You don't give because the Holy Spirit isn't leading you to give. Manifestations of agape love are no guarantee that the Holy Spirit will always lead the believer to give.

# Chapter 20

# Agape Love, Philos Love, and Appreciation

To simplify the flow of writing and reading this chapter, the words "he, his, him" should be understood generically as referring to both male and female.

A distinction must be made between agape love, philos love, and appreciation. They are not synonymous.

> agape love: an *unemotional respect* for another person's freedom to pursue his own internalize goal as long as the pursuit of that goal does not interrupt another person's freedom to pursue his goal.
> philos love: rapport and compatibility between two or more persons or between a human being and God, *permitting emotion* in both instances.

Having accepted these two definitions, I found myself in conflict. Conflict is defined as wanting two incompatible goals to be realized simultaneously. My conflict was between the definitions I had accepted as true and a new believer expecting me to accept as true that he really loves God because God has saved him. I wanted to believe my definitions and I wanted to believe the new believer's assertion, but the two were in conflict. Both cannot be true simultaneously. Either my definition had to be changed or what the new believer was expressing as love for God was not really love for God.

I accept as possible and reasonable that a new believer can describe his salvation experience emotionally; however, to call this emotionally bent statement "love for God" was impossible for me to accept because of the conflict between my definition and the new believer's statement. The new believer's relationship with God cannot be explained in terms of philos. He doesn't know enough about God to love Him with philos love; and if his stated love is emotional, it can't be agape love. How then can we explain this new Christian's emotion when it is attached to him telling us that he is loving God?

The light turned on and the answer became clear. The new believer's emotion is not attached to agape love or philos love. It is attached to something else perceived as love, called love, but not love, neither agape nor philos. The legitimate term used to explain this emotion is appreciation. The new believer, in response to his salvation, is expressing appreciation for the God who saved him, and his appreciation is filled with very positive emotion.

Appreciation is defined in the following manner: 1: a: a favorable critical estimate b: sensitive awareness; c: <u>an expression of</u> admiration, approval, or <u>gratitude</u> (Bingo!! light turns on-my comment here); 2: increase in value. (http://www.merriamwebster.com/dictionary/appreciation)

It is definition 1.c. that helped me: "<u>an expression of . . . gratitude</u>." This definition of appreciation explains the new believer's emotion that he expresses erroneously as his love for the God who saved him. Instead of an emotional "I really love Him for saving me," what he means is that he has an appreciation, a sensitive awareness of what has taken place in his life. God has saved him out of his total depravity. When clearly understood, that ought to be reason enough for anyone to become emotional.

Can a new believer actually "love God?" The answer is "yes." The new believer CAN manifest agape love for God, but philos love will have to wait for spiritual growth sufficient to know God through the internalization and actualization of absolute truth.

How can the new believer manifest agape love toward God in recognition of the salvation that he's received from Him? The new believer unemotionally respects God's right to have freely granted him eternal salvation as a totally depraved human being in response to his faith-alone in Christ-alone. Is it possible for him to manifest both agape love and appreciation simultaneously? The answer is yes. However, if emotion is attached to the acknowledgment, the acknowledgment is appreciation, not agape love. The manifestation of agape love is possible for a new believer, but not probable, because of two principles: 1) you can't do what you don't know how to do, no matter how sincere you might be; and 2) calling something by a specific name won't make it what it isn't. It is probable that the new believer will appreciate God long before he ever learns to love Him with either agape love or philos love.

Agape love is agape love. Philos love is philos love; and appreciation is appreciation.

# Section 7

# Freedom and the Christian Way of Life

# Chapter 21

# The Concept of Freedom

Freedom is vital to the Christian way of life because it is the environment in which every Christian decision has been decreed to be made; therefore, freedom will be studied in this chapter.

## Freedom and the Declaration of Independence

The following statement appears in the United States *Declaration of Independence* signed on July 4, 1776:

> "We hold these truths to be self-evident, that all men are created equal, that they are endowed by their Creator with certain unalienable Rights, that among these are Life, Liberty and the pursuit of Happiness."

## Freedom and the Constitution of the United States of America

The Preamble to the Constitution reads:

> "We the People of the United States, in Order to form a more perfect Union, establish Justice, insure domestic Tranquility, provide for the common defence, promote the general Welfare, and secure the Blessings of Liberty to ourselves and our Posterity, do ordain and establish this Constitution for the United States of America."

The following webpage[3] amplifies the phrase *and secure the Blessings of Liberty to ourselves and our Posterity.*

"Hand in hand with the general welfare, the framers looked forward to the blessings of liberty-something they had all fought hard for just a decade before. They were very concerned that they were creating a nation that would resemble something of a paradise for liberty, as opposed to the tyranny of a monarchy, where citizens could look forward to being free as opposed to looking out for the interests of a king. And more than for themselves, they wanted to be sure that the future generations of Americans would enjoy the same."

Posterity: posterity *n.* 1. Future generations. 2. All of a person's descendents.

# A Point of Clarification: Freedom vs. Responsible Freedom

Distinguish *freedom* from *responsible* freedom. Freedom that is not free is not freedom. Anything that infringes upon freedom destroys freedom at the point of infringement. The very nature of freedom necessitates the possibility that one person exercising his own personal freedom will infringe upon the freedom of another person. If that possibility is denied, then freedom has been redefined and that redefined form is no longer freedom.

Freedom intrinsically carries with it the possibility that when one person exercises his personal freedom that exercise may in fact infringe upon the personal freedom of another person. This is why the exercise of personal freedom ought to be *responsible* freedom.

*Responsible* freedom takes other people into consideration. *Responsible* freedom respects the personal freedom of others. *Responsible* freedom is the exercise of one's own personal freedom to the extent that it does not infringe upon the freedom of another person.

# Rhetorical Questions

I have some rhetorical questions that ought to be answered honestly. They will deal with freedom and its constituency; freedom and morality; freedom and right and wrong; freedom and absolute truth; and freedom and religion. Let's begin with freedom and its constituency.

## Freedom and Its Constituency

Who among us understands the *meaning* of freedom? Who among us *desires* personal freedom? Who among us *enjoys* personal freedom? Who among us understands the meaning of freedom for *all?* If freedom is extended to *all* through our Constitution, does the word *all* include *all,* or does it exclude *some*?

## Freedom and Morality

What is *moral* and what is *immoral*? Under the principle of freedom, are not the definitions of *morality* and *immorality* relative to the individual, group, or organization that defines the terms? Unless a person is willing to acknowledge the existence of absolute truth, it seems that the only immoral act would be for one person to exercise his personal freedom in such a manner that he disturbs the freedom of another person. Morality would be the exercise of personal freedom in such a manner that another person's freedom is not disrupted.

## Freedom and Right and Wrong

Does freedom permit conflicting definitions or interpretations of what is *right* and what is *wrong*? Under freedom, who has the right to say what is *right* and what is *wrong*? Under freedom, does the one who thinks he is *right* have the right to impose his *rightness* on the perceived *wrongness* of others? Under what condition or conditions does a person, group, or organization have the right to impose *rightness* upon another?

## Freedom and Absolute Truth

Assume for a moment the existence of *absolute truth.* Does freedom permit the *denial* of its existence?

## Freedom and Religion

Does freedom permit the existence of different *religions*? Does freedom permit the existence of *different* religious beliefs? Does freedom permit *atheism* as an alternative to religion? Does freedom permit the notion that Christianity is a spiritual way of life rather than a religious way of life?

## Personal Freedom and Control of a Person

Personal freedom and being controlled by another are mutually exclusive. If controlled, then not free. If free, then not controlled. When one person controls another, the one in control usurps the personal freedom of the one being controlled and the degree of control is not the issue. Control in any degree negates personal freedom because the integrity of personal freedom has been violated.

## Personal Freedom and Environment Control

The word environment is used here to mean "any location," for example, locations such as your home, school, library, shopping center, athletic field, backyard, hallway, grocery store, or airplane seat.

Whoever might be in-charge of any environment is at liberty to control the environment over which he has charge. Environment control may begin with goal development. Goals describe the nature for which an environment is established. They also determine what an environment is not.

Every environment generally has established goals, whether written or unwritten, and goals by their very nature place limits on the personal freedom of those functioning within that environment. For example, while I am free to drive my car on the highway, the goals of a grocery store do not permit me to drive my car up and down its aisles. While I may be free to market my garden vegetables at the Farmer's Market, the goals of the local high school do not permit me to set up a market in its hallways. The very nature of goals limits personal freedom.

## Personal Freedom, Rules and Operational Procedures

Rules and operational procedures designate the boundaries of personal freedom within an environment. They support the integrity of an environment and move that environment in the direction of goal achievement. They set forth the boundaries within which personal freedom is free to function. When personal freedom violates a rule or operational procedure within an environment, it disrupts maintenance of or advance toward the environment's goals.

# Personal Freedom and Responsibility

Freedom implies personal freedom to do as one pleases, but not without consequence if the act is irresponsible. Responsible freedom is the function of personal freedom to achieve one's own goal without denying another person the freedom to successfully achieve his own personal goal. The responsible side of freedom takes into consideration the freedom of another person to achieve his own goals without disruption.

When two or more people are gathered together, they may have different goals. These goals may be expressed as their differing wants (goals). Freedom permits differing wants; however, responsible freedom does not permit the pursuit of one's want in such a manner that the pursuit violates the freedom of another person to pursue and achieve his own goal. Perhaps an example or two will help.

Assume that a classroom teacher is free to teach and classroom students are free to learn. Suppose that a boy student wants (has a goal) to gain the attention of a female classmate with whom he is enamored. He begins with a "Psst!" that draws the attention of several classmates away from the teacher's teaching. He has just violated the freedom of the teacher to teach and the freedom of his fellow classmates to learn. All three can achieve their goals if the boy student will simply wait until after class to contact the young lady.

Assume that parents have a goal of eight hours sleep each night and the teenage son has an adjoining bedroom. If the son plays his TV too loud in the middle of the night, interrupting his parent's sleep, he has used his freedom to play his TV, but has violated his parent's freedom to achieve their needed sleep. Both can achieve their goals if the son will simply lower the volume on his TV.

In both cases just cited, the function of one person's freedom violated the personal freedom of another. Irresponsible freedom could have been avoided if the young boy had simply waited until after class to contact the young lady, and the son had just turned down his TV's volume.

## Freedom Distorted

The concept of freedom becomes distorted under three conditions: 1) I am free, but you are not; 2) You are free, but I am not; and 3) Neither of us is free.

Freedom doesn't mean do it my way, nor does it mean do it your way. Freedom means you do it your way, and I'll do it my way just as long as your way doesn't disrupt my freedom to achieve my goal and my freedom doesn't disrupt your freedom to achieve your goal.

## Freedom and the Christian Way of Life

Freedom is related to the Christian way of life and the Christian way of life is related to the resolution of the angelic conflict. Since God the Father has decreed that Christians resolve their portion of the angelic conflict, this makes the concept of freedom vitally important to the born-again Christian. Christians need to exploit every legitimate means of protecting personal freedom, not only their own, but freedom for all.

# Chapter 22

# Freedom and the Angelic Conflict

Freedom is the only environment in which the angelic conflict can be resolved and God be declared a just winner. If God is found to be unfair to any degree in dealing with Satan and the fallen angels, the angelic conflict will terminate immediately, and Satan will be declared the winner and God loses. God's integrity must be maintained throughout the entire conflict or He loses the battle.

A common fallacy among humans is the perception that God punishes His creatures to change behavior for wrong-doing. God doesn't punish anyone for the purpose of changing behavior. Punishment is designed for justice, not to change behavior. The fallen nature of mankind has difficulty coming to grips with this notion. Let's explore it.

The following concepts are basic to our understanding of freedom and the angelic conflict. God is perfect. God has a plan. Because God is perfect, His plan is perfect. God's righteousness demands righteousness from His creatures. God's justice demands justice for His creatures. What God's righteousness demands, God's justice executes. God's justice blesses or curses.

God the Father, in eternity past, decreed a plan to create. The purpose of His plan was to glorify Himself through the manifestation of the unity of His attributes. His plan permits created beings to choose between intimate relationship and fellowship with Him or to go-it-alone without Him. Starting out with a relationship to and fellowship with God, angels were free to break the relationship and fellowship by choosing to violate any of His divine decrees. Satan and one-third of the angels chose to break the relationship and fellowship with their Creator. They did so by making decisions that violated His divine will for them as created beings. Adam and Eve did the same thing in the Garden of Eden. The initial consequence of violating God's will for both angels and humans was spiritual separation from their Creator. Spiritual separation is not punishment. It's the decreed consequence of a bad choice.

God doesn't wait around to see what type of choices His creatures will make. His omniscience has known from eternity past every decision of every creature-good or bad (remember, absolutes exist). When the consequences of choices are decreed and revealed by God beforehand, the consequence of creature choices cannot be considered punishment. Consequences are simply decreed extensions of creature choices. Justice says, "If that's what you want, this is what you'll get. Consequences associated with choices were revealed in advance to you. You made the choice, and you are reaping the consequence." If the consequence hurts, you can't blame God if you knew in advance what was going to happen. Amazing, isn't it? Just look for someone else to blame. How about God? What difference does it make that you might have known in advance the consequence of your own bad decision?

Freedom means the condition of being free from restraints or control; the right and power to act, believe, or express oneself in a manner of one's own choosing. It's synonymous with liberty.

Freedom is a function of volition, and volition implies freedom. Angels were created with volition. Adam and Eve were created with volition. Humans are born with volition. Volition, whether angelic of human, provides capacity for choices. Choices can be good or bad, right or wrong when standards have been predetermined.

Assume for a moment the existence of absolutes, and assume that absolutes are the decrees of God that express His righteous will for His creatures. If His desire was the flawless obedience of His creatures, He could have created both angels and humans with a single-poled volition-positive pole only. This means that angels and humans would have no alternative but to comply with His will because no other alternative existed. If His desire was total disobedience of His creatures, He could have created both angels and humans with a single-poled volition-negative pole only. This means that angels and humans would have no alternative but to totally reject His will because no other alternative existed.

Since God created both angels and humans with a double-poled volition, a positive pole and a negative pole, this implies that God had more in mind than to create and force angels and humans to comply with His will, either obediently or disobediently.

The Bible indicates that God created for the purpose of glorifying Himself through the manifestation of the unity of His attributes. His attributes: sovereignty, eternal life, love, *justice*, absolute righteousness, omnipotence, omniscience, omnipresence, immutability, and veracity.

It's the attribute of *justice* that brings the angelic conflict and human history into perspective with each other. Justice has the capacity to bless or curse. This being true, let's ask ourselves a question. Why would the justice of God curse anything unless there existed a divine will of a righteous and holy God that could be violated? Cursing from the justice of

God is the negative consequence of a predetermined decree. Blessing from the justice of God is the positive consequence of a predetermined decree. If a creature of God violates His will, the integrity of God requires the attribute of justice to execute a negative consequence because God has decreed a negative consequence for every violation of His will.

The very nature of God's justice implies divine will that can be violated. It also implies volition with a positive and negative pole rendering both angels and humans capable of violating that will since both angels and humans were created with volition. Of what value is the justice of God if all it does is measure out varying degrees of blessing?

God is perfect, therefore, anything He does is perfect. Since God authored a plan, His plan is perfect because He is perfect. In short, God the Father's plan included the creation of angels. Lucifer, one of those angels, rebelled against his Creator. He led 1/3 of the angels to follow after him in rebellion against their Creator. Lucifer and his angelic following were offered a message of salvation which they rejected; so, by a predetermined divine decree, the justice of God summarily sentenced the fallen angels to eternal separation from their Creator. Lucifer appealed his sentence; so, God created man lower than the angels. Mankind's responsibility - obedience to God's plan. The point is that if the lower creature would be obedient, the implication is that the higher creature could have been but wasn't, and God is justified in carrying out the sentence. Lucifer and his followers would become eternally separated from the Author of all creation.

Can you imagine God creating man with a one-poled volition? How would that affect freedom as it relates to the resolution of the angelic conflict? Can you imagine God telling Satan to watch man's decisions because they would vindicate Him in carrying out his sentence? Satan would appeal directly to God's justice if man were given volition with only one pole-whether positive or negative. If only positive, Satan would say, "Yeah, sure!! You give man volition with only a positive pole. Man responds obediently to Your will, and You say, 'Look there. Look at what man is doing.' You've gotta' be kiddin' God. That isn't fair, and You know it! You just violated the integrity of Your own justice. You lose and I win!" If, however, God had given man only a negative pole, Satan would say, "Yeah, sure!! You give man volition with only a negative pole. Man responds with total disobedience, and You say, 'Look there. None of you get it right,' and we all go to the lake of fire. You gotta' be kiddin' God. That isn't fair either, and You know it! You just violated the integrity of Your own justice. You lose and I win!"

Humans have no way of knowing the number of objections Satan raised regarding his sentence to the lake of fire; however, because of the nature of those objections, God saw fit to decree four different periods of human history known as dispensations, each dispensation having its own particular set of rules by which man was to be obedient to resolve the conflict.

Biblically, we know that by the time the Church Age is culminated, every objection raised by Satan will have been so satisfactorily answered that Satan's only rebuttal is violence during the Tribulation period that immediately follows the rapture of the Church. The Tribulation period is the most violent period of human history. If you're a born-again Christian, you won't be there during that time period. You'll already be in heaven by way of physical death or the rapture, whichever occurs first in your life.

If the angelic conflict is to be resolved in a manner consistent with the integrity of God, then freedom has to be the environment in which the resolution is carried out. Freedom demands volition with a positive and negative pole; and man, having been created lower than the angels must use his volition to act in obedience to the Father's plan for the dispensation in which he lives. Remember, positive volition toward the Father's plan resolves the angelic conflict. Negative volition merely prolongs its resolution, and since God is not working on a time schedule, the amount of time it takes to resolve the conflict in no way affects the purpose for which God created in the first place. As long as His immutable justice continues to measure out predetermined consequences toward both positive and negative volition, He continues to honor and glorify Himself by continuing to manifest the unity of His attributes. Isn't freedom wonderful! It's the environment in which the angelic conflict is being resolved. You are free to choose and the predetermined consequence follows.

# Section 8

# Christianity and Modern-day "Tongues"

# Chapter 23

# Tongues: Why They Ceased in AD 70

> 1 Corinthians 13:8 Love never fails; but if there are gifts of prophecy, they will be done away; **if there are tongues, they will cease;** if there is knowledge, it will be done away. (NASB)

**Thesis.** The spiritual gift of tongues ceased in AD 70 and everything that is being called tongues, today, is no more than "gibberish," a counterfeit of the original spiritual gift.

**Gibberish defined.** Webster's dictionary defines "gibberish" as rapid and incoherent talk; unintelligible chatter. ("gibberish," Webster's New World Dictionary of the American Language)

## Introduction

**Purposes.** The purposes of this chapter are as follows: 1) To set forth the truth about the biblical gift of tongues; 2) To expose the modern-day "tongues experience" as a counterfeit of the original spiritual gift; 3) To expose the modern-day "tongues speaker's" shallowness of Bible knowledge regarding the spiritual gift professed to be possessed; 4) To assist the serious Bible student in search for truth on the subject of tongues; and 5) To send a warning to the spiritually naive and those who lack knowledge of the Word of God.

**Two principles of reasoning.** If it can be shown that tongues ceased in AD 70, it logically follows that every modern-day "tongues experience" is invalid and counterfeit under the following two principles.

> Principle: Nothing is valid that is invalid.
> Principle: Given the existence of absolutes, a practice that is invalid is a counterfeit.

**The method of theology.** Inductive reasoning will be the major method used to expose the modern-day "tongues experience" as counterfeit.

Lewis Sperry Chafer, a very notable theologian, in Volume 1, page 8, of his work entitled, *Systematic Theology*, writes that inductive reasoning is the theological method used in dealing with the truths of God's Word, and that induction gathers biblical facts on a given subject and then reduces those facts into one harmonious and all-inclusive statement. He also differentiates between perfect and imperfect inductions.

**Inductive reasoning.** Inductive reasoning draws conclusions from known facts. Inductions may be perfect or imperfect.

**Perfect induction.** Two things result in a perfect induction. 1) A perfect induction must consider every pertinent fact on the subject under consideration, and 2) Every fact must be interpreted correctly. To say that one has drawn a perfect induction implies that the conclusion reached is correct.

**Imperfect induction.** Two things result in an imperfect induction. 1) An imperfect induction results from failure to consider every pertinent fact on the subject under consideration, or 2) It may result from the misinterpretation of just one fact known about the subject. To say that one has drawn an imperfect induction implies that the conclusion reached is incorrect.

Succinctly stated, tongues was a temporary gift that operated from the day of Pentecost, AD 30 until AD 70, and any attempt to justify the practice of biblical tongues after AD 70 is biblically unjustified. Those who oppose this position frequently say, "But the Bible says . . . ," and then a passage of Scripture is quoted to justify the present day use of the gift of tongues. The implication is that a scriptural quote is all that is necessary to justify whatever we want to justify. This is spiritual nonsense and begs the question. We know what the Bible says, but the questions are these. What does it mean and how does it apply? And until there is an honest attempt to answer these two questions, spiritual chaos and confusion will continue to run rampant within the present day universal church. In view of the present day spiritual chaos and confusion, the following question is asked. Who among us is willing to listen to the prophet Isaiah? "Come now, and let us reason together, saith the LORD: . . ." (Isaiah 1:18 KJV)

**Three important dates:** There are three important dates in Bible history that impact a correct understanding of the biblical gift of tongues. The three dates are Pentecost AD 30, AD 70, and AD 96.

> **Pentecost AD 30.** This is the day in Acts 2 on which the biblical gift of tongues began to be exercised as a warning to unbelieving Israel of the impending fifth cycle of discipline.
>
> **AD 70.** This is the year in which God used the 5th cycle of discipline to drive the Jews out of their homeland because of their disobedience. This is well documented in secular history. The Jews are not scheduled to return legitimately to their homeland until the second coming of Christ.
>
> **AD 96.** This date represents the year in which the Christian canon of scripture was completed. The canon became complete the moment the Apostle John finished writing the Book of Revelation on the island of Patmos in AD 96.

**Israel during the lifetime of Jesus Christ.** Israel was already under the 4th cycle of discipline when Jesus was born. Approximately 70 years later, Israel would undergo the 5th cycle of discipline.

**Simple question! Simple answer?** The simple question is this. If tongues ceased in AD 70, then why did they cease in AD 70? It took less than five seconds to ask that question, and most people want an answer in the same amount of time, however, it doesn't work that way. If a person is interested in knowing why tongues ceased in AD 70, then there must be a willingness to hear all the facts so that a perfect induction can be drawn. Let's look at the facts.

# Fact #1

### The Five Cycles of Discipline: Leviticus 26:16-38

The five cycles of discipline are five different levels of divine discipline directed toward the nation of Israel for its failure as a nation to listen to God's warning, and the warning reads as follows:

> **Leviticus 26:14 But if you** [Israel] **do not obey Me** [God] **and do not carry out all these commandments** [as found in the Mosaic Law],
>
> **Leviticus 26:15 if, instead, you** [Israel] **reject My** [God] **statutes, and if your** [Israel] **soul abhors My** [God] **ordinances so as not to carry out all My** [God] **commandments, {and} so break My** [God] **covenant,**
>
> **Leviticus 26:16 I** [God]**, in turn, will do this to you** [Israel]**:**

The five cycles of discipline are listed in the following verses:

1st cycle: Leviticus 26:16-17
2nd cycle: Leviticus 26:18-20
3rd cycle: Leviticus 26:21-22
4th cycle: Leviticus 26:23-26
5th cycle: Leviticus 26:27-38; amplified in Deuteronomy 28:49-67

The five cycles of discipline were administered by God to Israel on the following occasions:

1. Northern Kingdom of Israel: 721 BC; Hosea 4:1-6; prophesied by Elijah, Elisha, Amos and Hosea.
2. Southern Kingdom of Israel: 586 BC; lasted 70 years.
3. Judea: AD 70; prophesied by Jesus in Luke 21:20-24.

Grace always precedes the fifth cycle of discipline. The first four cycles of discipline are grace warnings. In the fifth cycle of discipline, you either are killed or become enslaved.

**Conclusion.** The five cycles of discipline are a part of God's program for Israel.

# Fact #2

**A Prophetic Warning to Israel: Isaiah 28:11**

> **Isaiah 28:11 Indeed, He** [God] **will speak to this** [specifies a specific group of people; remember the word "this" when you read and interpret 1 Corinthians 14:21] **people** [Israel as a nation; not the church; not Christians, but Israel and Israel alone] **through stammering lips** [speech that when miraculously spoken by persons who had never learned the language make the speakers sound like drunkards] **and a foreign tongue** [all tongues were Gentile languages],

This passage is both a prophecy and a warning. As prophecy, it anticipates the beginning of tongues on the Day of Pentecost, AD 30, and as a warning it anticipates the fifth cycle of discipline to Israel in AD 70.

It is extremely important to note from this prophecy that God was going to use stammering lips and a foreign tongue to speak to THIS PEOPLE, that is, Israel as a nation, and if we are not impressed by this important point, the impact of 1 Corinthians 14:21 will be missed.

**Conclusion.** While some members of the church possessed the gift of tongues, the impact of the gift was upon THIS PEOPLE, that is, Israel as a backslidden nation.

# Fact #3

**Israel's Backsliddenness and Its Form: Arrogance and Drunkenness: Isaiah 28:1-11**

> **Isaiah 28:1 Woe to the proud crown** [arrogance] **of the drunkards** [drunkenness] **of Ephraim, And to the fading flower of its glorious beauty, Which is at the head of the fertile valley of those who are overcome with wine!**
>
> **Isaiah 28:2 Behold, the Lord has a strong and mighty agent** [a foreign power used as God's tool for carrying out the fifth cycle of discipline against Israel]**; As a storm of hail, a tempest of destruction, Like a storm of mighty overflowing waters, He has cast it** [Israel] **down to the earth with His hand.**

**Isaiah 28:3** The **proud crown** [arrogance] **of the drunkards** [drunkenness] **of Ephraim is trodden under foot.**

**Isaiah 28:4 And the fading flower of its** [Israel's] **glorious beauty, which is at the head of the fertile valley, will be like the first-ripe fig prior to summer; which one sees, and as soon as it is in his hand, He swallows it.**

**Isaiah 28:5 In that day the Lord of hosts will become a beautiful crown and a glorious diadem to the <u>remnant of His people</u>** [Jewish believers not backslidden].

**Isaiah 28:6 A spirit of justice for Him who sits in judgment, a strength to those who repel the onslaught at the gate.**

**Isaiah 28:7 And these also <u>reel with wine</u> and <u>stagger from strong drink</u>: The priest and the prophet** [the Bible teachers of that day] **<u>reel with strong drink</u>, They** [the Bible teachers of that day] **are <u>confused by wine</u>, they** [the Bible teachers of that day] **<u>stagger from strong drink</u>; they** [the Bible teachers of that day] **reel while having visions, They totter when rendering judgment.**

**Isaiah 28:8 For all the tables are full of filthy vomit** [sick from too much drinking], **without a single clean place** [vomit is everywhere].

**Isaiah 28:9 "To whom would He** [God] **teach knowledge? And to whom would He** [God] **interpret the message? Those just weaned from milk? Those just taken from the breast?**

**Isaiah 28:10 "For He** [God] **says, '<u>Order on order, order on order</u>** [teaching doctrine categorically, that is, selecting various Bible subjects and teaching all the Bible has to say about those subjects], **<u>line on line, line on line</u>** [teaching the Word of God a word at a time and declaring the meaning of each word], **<u>a little here, a little there</u>**

[selecting a timely message from an appropriate text wherever it may be found]."

**Isaiah 28:11 Indeed, He** [God] **will speak to this people** [Israel] **through stammering lips** [the spiritual gift of tongues that when miraculously spoken makes the speaker sound like a drunkard] **and a foreign tongue** [this reference to tongues is a reference to Gentile languages],

**Conclusion.** At the time of this writing, Israel as a nation was overcome with arrogance and drunken backsliddenness.

# Fact #4

**Paul States the Purpose of Tongues: 1 Corinthians 14:22**

**1 Corinthians 14:22 So then tongues are for a sign, not to those who believe, but to unbelievers; but prophecy is for a sign, not to unbelievers, but to those who believe. (KJV)**

Has anyone ever stopped long enough to ask either of the following questions? What was the purpose of tongues? What did God want to accomplish through the spiritual gift of tongues? The answers to these questions become clear when 1 Corinthians 14:21 is compared with 1 Corinthians 14:22.

1. Tongues were for a *sign*. (v.22)
2. Tongues were for a sign to *unbelievers*. (v. 22)
3. Tongues are directed toward *Jews*. (v. 21)

**First Conclusion:** Tongues were a sign to unbelieving Israel.

**Second Conclusion:** Tongues were a sign to unbelieving Israel of the impending fifth cycle of discipline. Remember, they were already under the fourth cycle at the time of Paul's writing.

# Fact #5

## 1 Corinthians 14:21. The Purpose of Tongues Is Related to Isaiah 28:11

> **1 Corinthians 14:21 In the Law it is written** [a reference to Isaiah 28:11], **"By men of strange tongues and by the lips of strangers I will speak to this** [the word "this" is the same word used in Isaiah 28:11 and is a reference to Israel as a nation; not the church; not Christians, but Israel as a nation; in other words, "Jews"] **people** [Israel]**, and even so they** [Israel] **will not listen to Me," says the Lord.**

If the purpose for the gift of tongues is to be understood, the relationship between Isaiah 28:11 and the spiritual gift of tongues must be understood. This passage links the Church Age gift of tongues to Israel as a nation, herein, referred to as "*this people*." It should be strongly emphasized that the phrase "*this people*" in Isaiah 28:11 refers exclusively to Israel as a nation.

**Conclusion.** Some members of the Church will possess the gift of tongues, but God designed the *benefit* of the gift to be for Jews, not the church, not Christians, but Jews, and any attempt to teach otherwise does injustice to the Word of God.

# Fact #6

### Tongues Will Cease: 1 Corinthians 13:8

> **1 Corinthians 13:8 Love never fails; but if there are gifts of prophecy, they will be done away;** *if there are tongues, they will cease*; **if there is knowledge, it will be done away. (KJV)**

Prophecy and knowledge and tongues are spiritual gifts, and from this verse, three things are evident about these spiritual gifts:

1. prophecy (as a gift) will be done away.
2. tongues (as a gift) will cease.
3. knowledge (as a gift) will be done away.

Note the following things about these three phrases.

1. Both prophecy and knowledge "will be done away," but tongues "will cease."
2. The verb used with both prophecy and knowledge are the same.
3. The verb used with tongues is different.

Now, let's examine these three phrases as they exist in the Greek manuscript from which they are translated:

| **Gift** | **Terminology** |
|---|---|
| prophecy | will be done away |
| προφητεῖαι | καταργηθήσονται |
| tongues | will cease |
| γλῶσσαι | παύσονται |
| knowledge | will be done away |
| γνῶσις | καταργηθήσεται |

It should be clear from these three phrases that prophecy, tongues and knowledge are temporary gifts; however, we are not told when these three gifts will cease to function, and we are not told why they will cease to function. The *when* and *why* will be discussed later in this chapter.

Now let's examine the grammatical construction of the verbs used to indicate the temporary nature of these three gifts.

| **prophecy** | **tongues** | **knowledge** |
|---|---|---|
| καταργηθήσονται | παύσονται | καταργηθήσεται |
| 3rd person plural | 3rd person plural | 3rd person singular |
| future passive indicative | future passive indicative | future **middle** indicative |

There are two major and significant differences in the three verbs used to indicate the temporary nature of these three spiritual gifts:

1. The root verb used with the temporary gift of tongues is different from the root verb used with the other two temporary gifts.
2. The verb used with tongues is in the "middle voice" while the verb used with both prophecy and knowledge is in the "passive voice."

What is the significance of the middle voice as opposed to the passive voice?

1. The middle voice, used with tongues, indicates that the gift of tongues would work against itself to bring about its own termination.

**Application.** Since tongues were a sign, when the sign had served its full purpose, the sign would no longer be needed, therefore, tongues had a limited use from the beginning, and when their usefulness had run its course, tongues ceased in and of themselves.

2. The passive voice, used with prophecy and knowledge, means that the subject receives the action of the main verb.

**Application.** Both prophecy and knowledge received the action of termination by being worked upon by an outside force. The outside force was the completed canon of scripture, so, when the canon of scripture became complete, namely, after the Apostle John received the Book of Revelation from the Lord Jesus Christ on the island of Patmos in AD 96, the gifts of prophecy and knowledge were no longer needed, therefore, the completed canon of scripture became the outside force that rendered both prophecy and knowledge no longer necessary.

**Conclusion.** Since the gift of tongues was a sign of the impending fifth cycle of discipline to Israel, tongues ceased the moment Israel was driven out of her land under the fifth cycle of discipline in AD 70, therefore, every modern-day form of tongues is a spurious counterfeit of the original gift and does not have its source in God.

# Fact #7

**God Used Titus to Administer the Fifth Cycle of Discipline to Israel in AD 70**

The fact that God used Titus to administer the fifth cycle of discipline to Israel in AD 70 is a well documented fact, even in profane history. For example, one encyclopedia reads, "Titus Flavius Sabinus Vespasianus (c. AD 40-81), Roman emperor, son of Vespasian, was born in Rome, December 30, 40 or 41. He served in Germany and Britain and commanded a Roman legion in Vespasian's campaign against the Jews, directing the campaign in Judea in 69; he took Jerusalem, September 8, to, after a long siege, and on his return to Rome he was rewarded with the title of Caesar and was given a part in the government." (Collier's Encyclopedia, 1956, Volume 18, p. 586)

## Fact #8

### If Tongues (plural) Ceased in AD 70, All Forms of Tongues Ceased in AD 70

In an attempt to respond to the conclusion that tongues ceased in AD 70, some have advanced the argument that there are different types of tongues, and only tongues similar to those of Acts 2 have ceased. Tongues, in Acts 2, are said to be the miraculous ability to preach the gospel in a language never learned, and not understood by the preacher, yet understood by the hearer. Tongues, in 1 Corinthians 14, are said to be the Christian's prayer language, which language is foreign to the person exercising the gift, but understood by God. This argument allows for one form of tongues to be terminated in AD 70, while allowing another form to continue. How does one answer the argument that only the Acts 2-type of tongues ceased in AD 70?

1 Corinthians 13:8 says, ". . . whether there shall be tongues, they shall cease." Here, the pronoun "they" is plural and correctly reflects the plural number of its antecedent plural noun "tongues." Since "tongues" is plural, this verse, by direct statement, prophesies a future cessation of the multiple and varied forms of tongues, therefore, it is proper to make the following inquiry. If the Bible prophesies the cessation of the multiple and varied forms of tongues, when will this cessation occur? The answer is quite easy. All forms of tongues ceased in AD 70. And why? Because tongues were a sign to unbelieving Israel of the impending 5th cycle of discipline, and when the 5th cycle of discipline occurred in AD 70, the need for the sign no longer existed, and therefore ceased in every form.

## Fact #9

**Apology or Polemic? 1 Corinthians 12-14**

The issue regarding chapters 12 and 14 of 1 Corinthians is whether these two chapters are a tongues *apology* or a tongues *polemic*. An apology is an argument that builds a case in favor of something. A polemic is an argument that builds a case against something. A close and careful study of these two chapters indicates their polemic nature as Paul builds a case against the abuse of tongues in the Corinthian church. When the polemic nature of 1 Corinthians 12 and 14 is understood, then and only then, can 1 Corinthians 12:39 be translated and interpreted correctly.

**Conclusion.** 1 Corinthians 12-14 is a POLEMIC against the abuse of tongues in the Corinthian church.

# Fact #10

**Should Tongues Really Be Coveted? 1 Corinthians 12:31**

**1 Corinthians 12:31 But covet earnestly the best gifts: and yet shew I unto you a more excellent way. (KJV)**

This verse presents a problem for anyone who is translating from the original Greek language. The very first word in the Greek sentence is the word ζηλοῦτε (zeloute), and here's the problem. This word can be correctly translated in three different ways.

ζηλοῦτε second person plural, present active imperative
ζηλοῦτε second person plural, present active subjunctive
ζηλοῦτε second person plural, present active indicative

Each of these grammatical constructions has its own translation. For example:

ζηλοῦτε second person plural, present active imperative

> The imperative mood is a command, and this translation would demand the force of a command. Unfortunately, this word is translated as a command in the English King James Version, the English New American Standard Version and the English New International Version and Living Letters. Each reads as follows:

King James: "covet earnestly"
New American Standard: "earnestly desire"
New international Version: "eagerly desire"
Living Letters: "try your best to get"

ζηλοῦτε second person plural, present active subjunctive

The subjunctive mood recognizes the free will of the individual and then points them in a desired direction. Unfortunately, this word is translated in this manner in the New English Bible. It reads as follows:

New English Bible: "you should aim at"

ζηλοῦτε second person plural, present active indicative

No English version of the Bible translates this verb to reflect the indicative mood. To reflect the indicative mood, this verb would be translated in the following manner:

King James: "you are coveting earnestly"
New American Standard: "you are earnestly desiring"
New International Version: "you are eagerly desiring"
Living Letters: "you are trying your best to get"

Only the indicative mood properly reflects the polemic nature of 1 Corinthians 12 and 14. The polemic nature, then, demands that 1 Corinthians 12:31 be understood as Paul exposing a problem in the church at Corinth, namely, the abuse of the gift of tongues. He was not commanding them to seek after a specific gift, namely, tongues.

It is interesting that a footnote on 1 Corinthians 12:31 in the New International Version is the only reference in any modern English version wherein an appropriate translation is rendered. This footnote reads as follows:

New International Version: "But you are eagerly desiring"

**Conclusion.** 1 Corinthians 12:31 does not command present day believers to seek the gift of tongues. In fact, when properly translated, this verse accuses the Corinthian believers of wrongfully seeking the tongues gift.

# Fact #11

**Forbid Not to Speak in Tongues. 1 Corinthians 14:39**

> **1 Corinthians 14:39 Therefore, my brethren, desire earnestly to prophesy, and do not forbid to speak in tongues. (KJV)**

This verse is used as an argument to reject the idea that tongues ceased in AD 70. The argument follows this line. If tongues ceased in AD 70, then why did Paul tell the Corinthians to "forbid not to speak in tongues?"

The answer to this objection is quite easy. The Book of 1 Corinthians was written by the Apostle Paul in approximately AD 55, and the fifth cycle of discipline did not fall upon Israel until AD 70; therefore, at the time Paul wrote 1 Corinthians 14:39, tongues were still valid, and would be valid for another fifteen years.

**Conclusion.** This verse has no application for the Church today, and its validity for application to the Church ended in AD 70 when Israel was removed from her land by God under the fifth cycle of discipline.

# Fact #12

**To Correct Ancient Abuses Does Not Validate Tongues for Today**

1 Corinthians 14 is thought by some to be a chapter designed by the Apostle Paul to correct the abuse of tongues during his time. To acknowledge that chapter 14 is set forth to correct ancient abuses does not imply that any modern-day use that follows Paul's guidelines validates that present day use. 1 Corinthians 14 was set forth to correct ancient abuses only for that period of time in which tongues were valid. At the moment tongues ceased in AD 70, the need for chapter 14's corrective measures were no longer required.

# Fact # 13

**Associative Relationship vs. Causal Relationship: (Acts 2)**

1.  Remember that the tongues phenomena was prophesied in Isaiah 28:11. It began its fulfillment on the day of Pentecost, AD 30. This historical event is recorded for us in Acts 2, and after a thorough study of the passage, it becomes clear that three significant things happened simultaneously in the lives of those who were in that upper room. Let's look at those three things.

    A.  First, they became permanently indwelt with the Holy Spirit. This permanent indwelling of the Holy Spirit was prophesied by John the Baptist in Matthew 3:11.

    **Matthew 3:11 I** [John the Baptist] **indeed baptize** [identify] **you** [repentant Jews who came to John for water baptism] **with water unto repentance: but** [a conjunction of contrast, contrasting John's baptism of repentance and Jesus' baptism with the Holy Spirit] **he** [Jesus] **that cometh after me** [John the Baptist] **is mightier than I** [John the Baptist], **whose** [Jesus] **shoes I** [John the Baptist] **am not worthy to bear: he** [Jesus] **shall** [indicates a future time, specifically, the day of Pentecost, AD 30.] **baptize** [this word means "identify"] **you** [refers to Jews, specifically, those in the upper room in Acts 1:15] **with the Holy Ghost** [Greek: πνευμα (pneuma) meaning "Spirit"], **and with fire** [the baptism with fire will not occur until the second coming of Christ at which time every unbeliever on planet earth will be cast into hell fire, thereby identifying them with the fire of hell]: **(KJV)**

    B.  Second, they were filled with the Holy Spirit (Acts 2:4).

    **Acts 2:4 And they were all filled with the Holy Spirit . . .**

    This is the Greek phrase πιμπλημι (pimplemi) plus the genitive of πνυεμα (pnuema), which means that the Holy Spirit was the content of the filling, that is, it was the Holy Spirit with which the believers were being filled.

    C.  Third, they spoke in tongues.

2.      Now, since they were simultaneously indwelt by the Spirit, and filled with the Spirit, and spoke in tongues, the common error is to conclude that there must be a cause and effect relationship between these three phenomena. For example, just because they were filled with the Spirit and simultaneously spoke in tongues, this does not mean that the filling **caused** them to speak in tongues. Being filled with the Holy Spirit is what empowered them to speak in tongues, just as this same filling with the Holy Spirit empowered other believers prior to Pentecost, AD 30 to accomplish supernatural service for God. In addition, it is equally wrong to conclude that since they were indwelt with the Spirit, and simultaneously spoke in tongues, the indwelling of the Spirit **caused** them to speak in tongues.

3.      An acceptance of these fallacious cause and effect arguments leads to further erroneous conclusions. For example, it is wrong to conclude that if you have not spoken in tongues, you are not indwelt with the Holy Spirit. It is equally wrong to conclude that if you have not spoken in tongues, you are not saved. Both of these conclusions are wrong because they are based upon the fallacious notion that there is a cause and effect relationship between the indwelling of the Spirit and speaking in tongues, or a cause and effect relationship between the filling with the Spirit and speaking in tongues.

4.      What, then, really happened on the day of Pentecost, AD 30? Three things occurred simultaneously on that day. The upper room believers became permanently indwelt with the Holy Spirit; they became filled with the Spirit; and they spoke in tongues. It cannot be denied that these three phenomena occurred simultaneously, however, the relationship among these three phenomena is associative rather than causal, and there is a vast difference between an associative relationship and a causal relationship.

5.      What, then, is meant by an associative relationship? An associative relationship simply acknowledges that the indwelling of the Holy Spirit, the filling with the Spirit, and speaking in tongues were associated with one another on the day of Pentecost, AD 30. However, it is spiritually devastating to assume that there must be a cause and effect relationship between things associated with one another. Let me illustrate the foolishness of such an argument. If I see and hear a man singing while he is simultaneously playing a guitar, and he is simultaneously accompanied by a backup group of singers, should I conclude that the guitar is causing him to sing, or should I conclude that the backup group is causing him to sing. Obviously not!

But we can say that the man's singing is associated with guitar playing, and associated with a group of backup singers.

6. In this same manner, the permanent indwelling of the Holy Spirit, and the filling with the Spirit, and speaking in tongues were associated with one another on the day of Pentecost, AD 30, but not one of these three phenomena were the cause of any one of the other. The indwelling of the Holy Spirit was the fulfillment of prophecy, decreed in eternity past to be initiated on the day of Pentecost AD 30. The filling with the Spirit was a temporary empowerment which allowed those in the upper room to perform some form of supernatural service for God. Speaking in tongues was the fulfillment of prophecy, decreed in eternity past to be initiated on the day of Pentecost, AD 30; and again, while these three phenomena were associated with one another, not one of them was the cause of any other.

# Fact #14

**Reality vs. Validity**

Many modern-day "tongues" speakers appeal to their "tongues-experience" and argue for the validity of modern-day "tongues" based upon the reality of their own personal experience. It should be understood that reality is not always associated with validity. Something can be real, but not valid. For example, gossip is very real to its victim, but gossip is not a valid form of Christian activity. Bigotry is very real to its victim, but bigotry is not a valid Christian attitude. The point is simply this. Reality does not always imply validity, therefore, if someone tells you they have had a "tongues" experience, you may not be able to deny the *reality* of that experience, but you have every right, based upon the Word of God, to deny the *validity* of that experience.

# Fact #15

**Further Information About Reality vs. Validity**

The reader should understand the following: 1) The modern-day "tongues-experience" is not limited to Christianity. Other world religions have a similar manifestation, and since the adherents of other religions are considered unbelievers by God, it becomes evident that even unbelievers "speak-in-tongues." Obviously, no thoughtful Christian would attempt to equate the reality of this pagan phenomenon with the Christian gift of tongues. Real, yes. Valid, no! 2) Even unbelievers performed miraculous works for which they received the rebuke of Jesus in Matthew 7:21-23.

> **Matthew 7:21 "Not everyone who says to Me, 'Lord, Lord,' will enter the kingdom of heaven; but he who does the will of My Father who is in heaven.**
>
> **Matthew 7:22 "Many will say to Me on that day, 'Lord, Lord, did we not prophesy in Your name, and in Your name cast out demons, and in Your name perform many miracles?'**
>
> **Matthew 7:23 "And then I will declare to them, 'I never knew you; depart from Me, you who practice lawlessness.' (NAS)**

The reality of the fact that these unbelievers had cast out demons in the name of Jesus did not validate them as believers in the Lord's eyes. Obviously, this reality did not mean validity to Jesus, and if reality does not always imply validity to Jesus, why should reality always imply validity to you and me today? 3) During the Tribulation, that is, that period of human history between the rapture of the Church and the second coming of Christ, the dictator of the Revived Roman Empire, also known as the Anti-christ, will come with all power, signs and false wonders in accord with the activity of Satan (2 Thessalonians 2:8-9).

> **2 Thessalonians 2:8 And then that lawless one** [the dictator of the Revived Roman Empire] **will be revealed whom the Lord will slay with the breath of His mouth and bring to an end by the appearance of His coming** [the second advent];
> **2 Thessalonians 2:9 that is, the one whose coming** [the Anti-christ] **is in accord with the activity of Satan, with all power and signs and false wonders** [power, signs, and false wonders refer to miraculous works done in the power of Satan by the Anti-christ], **(NAS)**

The reality of this power and these signs and false wonders does not make them valid in the eyes of the Lord. Obviously, the reality of this power and these signs and false wonders cannot and should not be equated with validity by any thoughtful Christian.

The reality of the modern-day "tongues" phenomena is being equated with validity. Obviously, no knowledgeable Christian will equate this modern-day "gibberish" with biblical tongues that were valid from Pentecost AD 30 until the day the Jews were driven out of their land under the 5th cycle of discipline in AD 70.

# Fact #16

**The Sources of Modern-day "Tongues"**

There are several sources of this gibberish known as modern-day "tongues." The sources are as follows: 1) the engastrimuthos demon, 2) emotion, and 3) auto-induction. Only the unbeliever "speaks in tongues" by means of the engastrimuthos demon. The believer speaks through emotion or auto-induction.

The word "engastrimuthos" is the Greek word εγγαστριμυθος (engastrimuthos) found in the Septuagint that translates the Hebrew word אב (OB) in Isaiah 8:19.

> **Isaiah 8:19 And when they shall say unto you, Seek unto them that have familiar spirits** ["familiar spirits" is the Hebrew word אב (OB) and the Greek word εγγαστριμυθος (engastrimuthos) and refers to a demon that controls the vocal chords of the one it indwells], **and unto wizards that peep, and that mutter: should not a people seek unto their God? for the living to the dead? (KJV)**

It is imperative to understand that only unbelievers can speak by means of the engastrimuthos demon.

Emotion is another source of modern-day "tongues." An individual can allow himself or herself to produce this gibberish by elevating his or her emotional state to the necessary personal level. The level of emotion required to produce the phenomena differs from person to person, and for some the emotional level required can be quite low and unobservable to onlookers.

Auto-induced "tongues" is yet another source of this modern-day gibberish. By auto-induction is meant the ability to produce this gibberish at will. It is turned-on and turned-off at will. It is learned and often follows the same pattern, that is, it sounds the same every time it is manifested.

# Inductive Conclusion

Sixteen tongues related facts have been presented in this chapter, and now, an inductive conclusion can be drawn by drawing some of these facts together.

1. Tongues were a *sign*. (1 Corinthians 14:22) Fact #4
2. Tongues were a sign to *unbelievers*. (1 Corinthians 14:22) Fact #4
3. Tongues were a sign to unbelieving *Israel*. (1 Corinthians 14:21) Fact #5 and Fact #2
4. Tongues were for a sign to unbelieving Israel of the *impending fifth cycle of discipline*. (Leviticus 26:16-38) Fact #1
5. Historically, the fifth cycle of discipline occurred to Israel in AD 70. (profane history documents this)
6. It was prophesied that all forms of *tongues would cease*. (1 Corinthians 13:8) Fact #6

**Two Legitimate Questions.**

1. Question #1: When Did Tongues Cease?
2. Question #2: Why Did Tongues Cease?

**Two Inductive Conclusions.**

1. Inductive conclusion #1: All forms of tongues ceased in AD 70.
2. Inductive conclusion #2: All forms of tongues ceased in AD 70 because tongues were a sign to unbelieving Israel of the impending fifth cycle of discipline, and when the fifth cycle of discipline occurred, the sign ceased because the purpose for which it was intended no longer existed.

**Final Comments.**

The spiritual gift of tongues ceased in AD 70 and everything that is called tongues, today, is no more than "gibberish." They are a counterfeit of the original spiritual gift, and quoting Scripture to justify any form of modern-day "tongues" discloses the "tongues" proponent as either naive, shallow, or without clear understanding of the Book to which the justifying appeal is made. Every validating argument is weightless when measured against the Word of God, and can be proven to be so. The worst deception of all is the appeal to personal experience. To deny that someone might have had a personal "experience" is absurd. The real question, however, relates to the source of that experience. Brethren, the modern-day "tongues" experience is a counterfeit of the original gift. Please, do not be deceived!

# Glossary

Words are important. Words are symbols used to communicate meaning. Sometimes a word may have more than one meaning, and if the meaning intended by the communicator is not understood by the listening audience, misunderstanding occurs. Sometimes a word may be used that is not known to the listening audience. Under this condition, the communicator's message may not be understood. For these reasons, definitions and descriptions are provided for a list of words and phrases found in this book. Agreement with the author's theological positions is not the goal. The fundamental question regards whether his message is understood. Agreement or disagreement is the reader's choice.

**absolutes.** Principles, promises, doctrines, techniques, rules for living, and operational procedures decreed by God.

**absorption.** To take (something) in; to soak up.

**ambassadorship.** The born-again Christian functioning in Christian service representing God before his fellow-man.

**angelic conflict.** A term used to describe the conflict between God and Satan that began in eternity past, the consummation of which will be in God's favor at the end of human history.

**angelic conflict (amplified).** The environment in which human history is carried out; the background against which every circumstance of life is to be understood, measured, and analyzed if the "why's" of life are to make any sense.

**attributes of the Godhead.** Sovereignty, eternal life, love, justice, absolute righteousness, omnipotence, omniscience, omnipresence, immutability, and veracity.

**believer.** Anyone who has manifested faith-alone in Christ-alone for spiritual salvation; a born-again Christian.

**body parts.** The various parts of the physical human body, both internal and external, for example: hands, feet, eyes, ears, heart, lungs.

**born-again Christian.** A human being who during the Church Age has believed the good news that Jesus Christ died, was buried, and rose again the third day, thus, making spiritual salvation available to all who will believe.

**Christendom.** The entire body of people following the Bible in one form or another, but not necessarily born-again.

**Church Age.** That period of time designated as one of the dispensations of human history; specifically, that portion of human history between the first stage of the Age of Israel and the Tribulation period.

**collocation.** An arrangement of words that commonly co-occur, such as rancid butter, bosom buddy, or dead serious.

**core beliefs.** A combination of all of the relational strategies and world views learned from the time of physical birth up to the time of becoming born-again.

**counterfeit.** An imitation of what is genuine.

**creatures.** Created beings such as angels and human beings.

**dichotomous.** Two parts; body and soul when referring to an unbeliever.

**dispensation.** A period of human history marked by its own specific set of rules by which those living in that period of history will participate in the resolution of the angelic conflict by acts of obedience in accordance with the rules.

**divine institutions.** The institutions of freedom, marriage, family, and nationalism decreed by God the Father to perpetuate human history until the angelic conflict is resolved.

**dominant.** The term used to describe a solution associated with one's belief system that has been placed on the launching pad of the soul's mentality awaiting the opportunity for application to a life situation.

**experiential forgiveness.** That form of forgiveness of personal sins received under the following conditions: 1) spiritual salvation that cancels every sin committed from the time of one's physical birth until the moment of spiritual birth; 2) confession of sins committed between the time of salvation and physical death or the rapture whichever occurs first.

**habit.** A recurrent, often unconscious pattern of behavior that is acquired through frequent repetition; an established disposition of the mind or character.

**heart.** The second section of the conscious mind that contains three major centers and four sub-centers in which data is stored.

**Holy Spirit.** The third Person of the Godhead responsible to reveal truth and restore persons who are separated from God the Father's plan.

**human body.** The physical body, the material part of the human being generated by the union of a male sperm and a female ovum from the moment of conception.

**human body parts.** Every anatomical part of the human body, internally and externally.

**human good.** That form of good accomplished when a human being is functioning from the source of his old-man; referred to as wood, hay, and stubble in 1 Corinthians 3:12.

**human history.** That period of time associated with human beings running from the creation of Adam and Eve in the Garden of Eden and concluding with the last day of the millennial reign of Jesus Christ on earth.

**human nature.** The fallen nature of human beings caused by the moral fall of Adam and Eve in the Garden of Eden whereby every human being except Jesus Christ is born spiritually separated from the Triune Godhead.

**human soul.** The real you; that part of the human being that lives forever; the only part of the human being that is guaranteed eternal existence after physical death whether that eternal existence continues in heaven or the lake of fire.

**human spirit.** The human spirit is a receptor organ capable of receiving spiritual communication from God the Holy Spirit who takes up residence in the human spirit the moment a human being becomes born-again. Today, God the Father's plan does not include clairvoyance (visions associated with the spirit world) or clairaudience (hearing audible voices from the spirit world). His plan revolves around the Holy Spirit communicating with the born-again believer by means of the human Spirit. Do not expect to hear a voice. Do not expect a vision. When the Holy Spirit is speaking to the born-again believer through the human spirit, the believer can accurately validate the experience in only one way, namely, "I just know that I know that I know" what the Holy Spirit is saying to my human spirit. The Holy Spirit speaks to the believer's human spirit and not to his physical ears.

**imply.** To suggest.

**inference.** To draw a conclusion.

**infusion.** The act of filling with something.

**integrity of God.** A combination of three attributes of God: His love, His absolute righteousness, His justice; synonymous with holiness, godliness.

**in the Spirit.** The spiritual sphere from which the born-again Christian executes the Christian way of life that produces the likeness of Christ in His humanity.

**judicial forgiveness.** God the Father's legal pronouncement that the entire human race stands forgiven of personal sins because of the spiritual death of Jesus Christ on Calvary's cross upon which He became the substitute for every member of the human race; the basis upon which no personal sin ever sends any human being to hell or the lake of fire.

**launching pad.** The spiritual heart's third major center serving as the location from which each dominant thought is applied to a circumstance of life.

**man.** Except where evident that the word is used for male gender, it is used generically for mankind, embracing both male and female members of the human race.

**new-man.** The personification of the soul that is yielded to the influence of the Holy Spirit.

**new-man function.** The application of new-man beliefs to the circumstances of life.

**new-man logic.** The divinely inspired rationale that justifies what the born-again Christian thinks, says, feels, and does when functioning from the source of my new-man.

**new-man thinking.** That system of belief that embraces the principles, promises, doctrines, techniques, rules for living, and operational procedures designed by God the Father to be believed and obediently applied from the source of the new-man to the circumstances of life.

**non-dominance.** The term used to describe a solution associated with one's belief system that is positioned in either the old-man or new-man clothes closet; not on the launching pad of the soul.

**old-man.** The personification of the soul that has yielded itself to the influence of the body's sinful nature.

**old-man function.** The application of core beliefs to the circumstances of life.

**old-man logic.** The rationale used to justify what is thought, felt, said, and done when functioning from the source of the old-man.

**old-sin-nature.** Synonymous with sinful nature; the fallen nature with which every human being is born that trends away from God rather than toward Him.

**old-man thinking.** Core beliefs which are a combination of all of the relational strategies and world views learned from the time of physical birth until the moment of salvation.

**old-man thinking (amplified).** Old-man thinking is less about bad theology than it is about a bad view of self related to past sins, mistakes, painful events and relational influences that formed the beliefs held in one's heart.

**"Operation KRRY".** An acrostic that stands for knowing, reckoning, reckoning, and yielding; a four step process decreed by God the Father that places the born-again Christian "in the Spirit."

**operational procedures.** Guidelines developed to insure the smooth operation of any organization that move it toward the achievement of its goals.

**organic connection.** Two things combining to function as one.

**personal sins.** Mental, verbal, and overt violations of God the Father's divinely revealed standards.

**post-canon.** After AD 96; the date after which the New Testament canon of scripture had become complete.

**post-salvation sin account.** After salvation, the account into which each personal sin is logged.

**priesthood.** That form of Christian royalty from which status born-again Christians represent themselves before God.

**rapture.** The event that terminates the Church Age when Christ returns in the air for every born-again Christian, living and dead, to take them to heaven in a resurrection body for an evaluation of their Christian works as each stands one-on-one before Jesus at the bema seat of Christ.

**relational strategies.** From physical birth to the new-birth, those things learned from relationships with parents and others that were based upon what works to receive attention from others, approval from others, acceptance from others, and love from others.

**sinful nature.** The genetically prepared nature of all human beings, Jesus Christ the exception, that trends every human being away from God the Father rather than toward Him.

**spiritual.** That form of life possessed by every born-again Christian because of union with Christ.

**spirituality.** The spiritual condition of every born-again Christian while functioning from the source of the new-man.

**strategy.** A plan designed to bring satisfactory resolution to a circumstance of life.

**subconscious.** That part of the mind below the level of conscious perception.

**transformation.** The process of spiritual growth wherein the born-again Christian moves from old-man function into new-man function.

**trichotomous.** Three parts; spirit, soul, and body when relating to the born-again Christian.

**unconscious mind.** The division of the mind in psychoanalytic theory containing elements of psychic makeup, such as memories or repressed desires that are not subject to conscious perception or control, but that often affect conscious thoughts and behavior.

**volition.** A characteristic of the human soul that by divine design is the basis for freedom because it has both a positive and negative pole that enables humans to make both good and bad decisions when those decisions are measured by the absolute standards of God's decrees.

**world view.** From the moment of physical birth until the new-birth, the manner in which the old-man views an historical event, how it should be understood, how it operates; a view that is in contrast with God's viewpoint.

**yielded.** A mental attitude of surrender either to the sinful nature or the Holy Spirit; the fourth step of "Operation KRRY" when surrendering to the Holy Spirit.

# Abbreviations

KJV    King James Version
NASB New American Standard Bible
NIV    New International Version
NKJV New King James Version
NLT    New Living Translation

# Endnotes

[1] http://www.barna.org/barna-update/article/5-barna-update/48-more-americans-are-seeking-net-based-faith-experiences?q=internet

[2] http://en.wikipedia.org/wiki/List_of_Christian_denominations

[3] http://en.wikipedia.org/wiki/List_of_Christian_denominations